Stop Pitching!

The Role of
Conversations
in the World of Sales

THE COVENANT GROUP

Stop Pitching!
Copyright © 2022 by Dean Harder.
All rights reserved.

Edited by John Donnelly

Book and cover design by Patrick Rasoanaivo

ISBN 978-1-7780724-0-6
ISBN 978-1-7780724-1-3 (ebook)
ISBN 978-1-7780724-2-0 (audio)

For my dad

Contents

CHAPTER 1: A Conversation, not a Pitch!   15

CHAPTER 2: Attracting & Engaging   19

CHAPTER 3: Compelled   27

CHAPTER 4: Doubly Good   39

CHAPTER 5: You, not me !   55

CHAPTER 6: Ready! Set! Go!   65

CHAPTER 7: Yes. No. Maybe.   89

CHAPTER 8: Scripting the Performance   95

CHAPTER 9: WHaa   113

CHAPTER 10: P-PASS   123

CHAPTER 11: Words Matter   135

Foreword

Have you ever met someone and felt a strong connection with them after talking just a few moments? How did that happen? What if there was a way to make that happen? Imagine how much easier your life as a sales professional would be if you knew how to open meaningful conversations with your ideal prospects, those you serve best? How much would that be worth to you? Most likely a lot.

The question to answer is, how do you turn a conversation into a human connection and then turn that connection into a relationship, and that relationship into a win-win? The answer is simple: read this book.

Dean Harder is a master of both the art and science of conversational selling. I could tell you of his achievements and credentials, but the most important thing to tell you is that Dean has engaged in over 21,000 sales conversations since 1998. You also need to know that he has been a Top Ten producer with one of the leading U.S. life insurance companies every year since 1999. He is a sought-after keynote presenter to life insurance industry audiences throughout North America, as well as a consultant and trainer to sales organizations, both inside and outside this industry. Dean is the real deal. For proof of his abilities, travel back in time with me to a Monday in late January 2020 at the Four Seasons Hotel Las Vegas.

I have just finished my third speaking assignment for a group of extremely successful sales professionals at Forum 400, an elite organization of top life insurance professionals throughout the United States. My daughter and business partner Jenny and I are standing at a meet-and-greet table signing up people for my Ultimate Speaking System speaking skills coaching program. One of those who comes over and hires me as his coach is Dean. After filling out the application, signing it and giving Jenny his credit card, Dean starts a conversation with me. What exactly does he say? Read this book and you'll learn what you can say and do to start your conversations, as well as design your conversational dialogues around helping those you serve get what they want.

Fast forward to Wednesday, the final day of the event. Dean is now like family, an old friend, a best buddy I have known for years. I have met tens of thousands of people and meeting Dean was the absolute highlight of the three-day event for Jenny and me. Keep in mind I'm a Hall of Fame professional speaker, having spoken over the past forty-five years at more than 3,000 events like the one I had just finished. Now, a long time later, Dean is still one of my favorite clients, as well as a friend.

What if you could master skills that would connect you to a man like me and a young woman like Jenny, forming a deep personal relationship? What would that do for you and your career in the world of sales? It could be a game changer, that's what it could do!

As you read this book, you will learn techniques and skills and gain insights that will improve your ability to attract, connect and relate to almost anyone. Get set to meet your soon-to-be good friend, conversation coach, as well as your conversational selling guide, Dean Harder.

Joel Weldon, creator of Joel Weldon's *Ultimate Speaking System*

Introduction

When relationships matter, so too does conversation. When I think back on my life and how others have influenced me, two people come to mind. The first is my friend Eric Hagman.

I met Eric in Bloomington, Minnesota in 1990. He and his wife Tracey were sitting in front of Jackie and me one Sunday morning in church. They turned around to say hello. They were friendly, non-threatening, interesting, interested, funny and easy to interact with. Eric and I shared many an early morning coffee at Perkins, the neighborhood coffeeshop, prior to the Hagman family moving permanently to Kenya to live and work. Eric is the ideal combination of a person who listens, hears, shares, challenges, encourages, admits shortcomings, gently points out fault, laughs, laughs at himself, oozes wisdom, learns, grows, and changes, all the while somehow staying the same genuine guy. In a nutshell, Eric is one of the most gifted conversationalists I've ever met.

Conversely, I have a long-time friend (who will go unnamed and for whom I care dearly) I'll call Steve. I can truly say that in the dozens of interactions Steve and I have shared over a lifetime there hasn't been a moment where it seemed like he really cared about what I felt, thought, had to say, or wanted to share. Steve loves the sound of his own voice. Even though he has tremendous experience, incredible knowledge, a great life story, and a strong dose of wisdom, I find myself exhausted nearly every time we chat.

Both men have been successful in life. So, what's the point of mastering the art of conversation if one can be successful regardless of method? Eric has been involved in business ventures where relationships were central to the success of his business. Steve has been a pitchman in business ventures where, frankly, relationships weren't critical to the outcome. When relationships matter, so too does conversation.

I think back to some of my teachers during my high school years in Mountain Lake, Minnesota, and easily recall wanting to sit in their classrooms[1]. (Like you, I can also quickly think of teachers I couldn't stand being in a classroom with.)

I recently did an exercise where I listed out a group of people's names under the heading of My Personal Mount Rushmore. I imagine most people reading this are familiar with the massive stone carving of four former U.S. presidents near Rapid City, South Dakota. My imaginary monument too has four names. Six of

---

[1] Thank you Tom Appel, Linda Mix and Sylvia Ekstedt.

my Top-20 names are those of teachers I had in my formative years. Frankly, that came as a surprise; not that there were former teachers, but that just over one-quarter of my Top-20 name list included teachers I had so many years ago.

From an early age I could easily differentiate between the two types of individuals (Erics and Steves). The sad part is I can also see myself having been both types at various points in my own life. I've been guilty of doing to others what I despise others doing to me. Knowing that I too am prone to error along the way, I continue to build my skills to engage others even more naturally.

So, I'd like to ask a simple question: Do you want to help people?

If you said, "No, I really don't want to help people," this book may not be worth the read. If, however, you said, "Yes! I love helping people!" then my hope is you will read on because this book has been written for you.

Your ability to connect quickly and deeply is at the core of helping people. Pitching a product or even an idea may have shades of 'helping others' embedded in the gizmo or the thought. Pitching, however, has a way of creating debate, negative tension and yuck-like feelings inside the person being pitched to.

So, let's see how the antidote to pitching is conversation. How about we get started?

One good conversation can shift the direction of change forever.

Linda Lambert

Chapter 1

A Conversation, not a Pitch!

Think back to an experience where you were sitting across the table from someone who clearly wanted to pitch you something. Perhaps it was the young woman you met waiting in line at the grocery story who's now at your home trying to pitch a new vitamin that promises to give you unexplainable energy. Maybe it was a nice man, a friend of a friend, who was pitching you a product you didn't really understand, so you weren't feeling good about signing up. Or maybe you were sitting through a time-share pitch with a very polished woman who nearly had you convinced it was a no-brainer, yet you really didn't know why. In the end, you passed on the vitamins, told the friend of a friend you'd think about it, or got up and walked out of the time-share pitch.

The point of this book is to suggest a better way—a much better way—for you and the people you serve to experience a favorable, even delightful, way to interact in the sales environment. This much better way is Conversational Selling.

For more than two decades I have been a thought leader in a field that found me. Over the years, I have come to realize that people want to be helped. Shoot, even I like to be helped when I don't have a clue of what's going on. You likely look to others for help, especially when it comes to something you struggle with or aren't sure about. This is not a novel idea. You generally look to others to help you make decisions, like when buying a car, purchasing a home, shopping for clothes, searching for a gift, remodeling your kitchen or figuring out how to make financial decisions for your future.

I'm going to bet it's equally obvious you don't like to feel manipulated or taken advantage of along the way. My most successful interactions have not been about pitching. No, my most successful interactions have been about interacting with another person inside a conversation that matters to them. It's about starting from the outside in.

When starting from the outside, you focus on the other person. Focusing on the other person is one of two key principles when it comes to influencing others. Starting from the outside and working in begins by attracting a person into a conversation that's meaningful to them—a conversation that's...well...about them.

I have been part of about 1,000 conversations a year since 1998. That means I have engaged in more than 21,000 conversations during that time, maybe more. Regardless of the actual number, the number of interactions is surely in the thousands.

In the early years, it would be a stretch to describe the interactions I had with others as conversations. In fact, it would be more than fair to describe those early interactions as all-out sales pitches.

Pitches are not evil, wrong or always misguided. More often than not, however, a pitch is not a pleasant experience. I've come to realize that conversational selling is a completely different mindset than giving sales pitches. In conversational selling the format, pacing, energy, tension and even word choices are quite different than the oft-scoffed, one-sided pitch many sales professionals are trained to give.

In the pages ahead you will learn the key differences between Pitching a Sale and Conversational Selling. You will read about conversational techniques you can use immediately in your own business, in your sales role or within your sales organization. You will feel more confident, more energized and even more motivated to move away from pitching your products and ideas to embracing conversational selling.

Are you ready to dive in?

Change the way you look at things and the things you look at change.

Wayne D. Dyer

Chapter 2

Attracting & Engaging

As a teenager one October Saturday in the early 1980s, I was helping my dad and my Uncle Glen harvest corn when one of the grain trucks broke down. Uncle Glen drove the grain truck to Lake Crystal where it could be repaired. I followed behind in a pickup truck so he would have a way of getting back to the farm.

When I pulled up to the front door of Crysteel Manufacturing, Uncle Glen was already walking out of the building toward me. I stopped the truck, jumped out the driver's side and started walking around to the passenger side to hop in, assuming Uncle Glen was going to drive us back home.

"Dean, jump back in and drive home!" he said with a smile before I reached the front of the truck.

I was sixteen, so those words made me feel like I was going to fly the Space Shuttle back to Earth from the heavens above! As we headed back down Minnesota Highway 60, Uncle Glen asked what I liked most about helping out on the farm that time of year. I told him the obvious, like being outside, driving tractors and grain trucks, chopping stalks and, especially, taking over the grain cart. I loved the smell of corn drying down at the bin site and the feeling of accomplishment when a field of corn disappeared and all that was left was the corn stock stubble. Uncle Glen asked me some questions about school and the various activities I was involved in. To say the conversation was about me is an understatement.

While I drove the pickup, my uncle drove the conversation. In a matter of just thirty minutes, I felt a new connection with my uncle.

"What do you want to do after high school—you know, with your life?" he asked when we were about fifteen minutes from home.

I can recall all this like it was yesterday. The first half-hour was what the *attraction* phase of a conversation looks likes, feels like, sounds like. The final fifteen minutes were what the engagement phase is all about.

While I had taken the steering wheel literally, Uncle Glen took it figuratively. He went on to share some of his own experiences with me after someone had posed a similar question to him back in his youth. The wisdom and advice he imparted to me on that drive home to Mountain Lake sticks with me to this day.

Way too often I feel pounced on by a salesperson. I sometimes wonder what that forty-five-minute ride home would have been like if Uncle Glen had jumped into the driver's seat himself rather than taking the passenger seat and having a conversation with me about my life. I feel people are too often more concerned about their own worlds, their own lives, their own families, their own jobs, their own careers, their own interests, their own hobbies, their own little universes.

It's not uncommon to get the feeling that many salespeople are most interested in making a sale, hitting their quotas or making it into some special recognition club, rather than focusing on helping the other person first. The best outcome may not be a sale that day. You may just land a lifelong client if you help them get what they want first.

So, how does one go about attracting others into a conversation?

Curiosity. Start by being curious about others.

Curiosity simply means having a strong desire to know or learn something. You may use words and phrases like *inquisitive, interested,* and *poke around a bit* to better understand what being curious means. The problem with curiosity is that it's too often a one-way street. Think about the person who walks into a car dealership and opens doors, peers inside vehicles, carefully reads the window stickers, and perhaps even lifts the hoods of the cars. It seems fair to say these are the actions of a curious person.

But what about the salesperson? How does curiosity play a part in attracting this potential customer into an engaging conversation? Does she say to the potential customer, "How about I show you some good deals out on the lot?" Or how about, "Did you know that today we have an additional one-thousand-dollar rebate on all new models that arrived just this week? But you have to buy a car today!"

I don't know about you, but either one of these questions directed at me is likely to snuff out any interest I may have had in chatting with this salesperson. For starters, when it comes to having a meaningful conversation between two people, I am convinced *the role of attraction is markedly different than the role of engagement.*

The differences between attraction and engagement may be subtle, yet from years of observing others in their roles helping me, and me in my own role of helping others, there is no doubt that a profound difference exists.

Highly successful entrepreneurs, salespeople, manufacturer's representatives, executives, senior leaders, teachers, and even parents, *attract others into meaningful conversation before they attempt to engage them.*

One of these highly successful entrepreneurs is my friend, Norm Trainor. For more than eight years I have been fortunate—no, blessed—to have a professional relationship with The Covenant Group, led by Norm, a well-seasoned coach to more than 35,000 advisors and agents throughout the world over the years. I'm one of those 35,000-plus. Just as a mother and a father are the sources of DNA for their newborn, Norm is one of my professional 'parents.' This book is a direct result of my learning and growing through hours and hours of self-study, group dialogue, self-reflection and, perhaps most impactful, conversations with Norm himself. Norm has an uncanny ability to attract others into conversations that lead to action.

The very first time I heard Norm speak was at a corporate event. By the time he had wrapped up his main platform presentation, I knew I wanted to know more. Norm inspired me as he shared several stories about how the work of The Covenant Group helps entrepreneurs and executives in the sales environment live the lives they always dreamed of living. In other words, nearly his entire message was about others, not about The Covenant Group. I was so intrigued that I immediately reached out to set up a one-on-one with Norm to find out more about The Covenant Group and how their work helped people live the lives they always dreamed of living.

Take a moment to read the last bit back to help highlight the distinct difference between attracting and engaging within a selling scenario. Norm didn't pitch what The Covenant Group did, he instead shared how The Covenant Group helps the people they serve get what they want.

Attract (verb) cause someone to have a liking for or interest in something; a curiosity.

Engage (verb) cause someone to become involved in a conversation or discussion.

Conversational selling is *about attracting others into conversations that matter to them.* Once someone is attracted—curious—then it's natural to engage them in dialogue around a topic you yourself have expertise in.

Basically, I have been compelled by curiosity.

Mary Leakey

Chapter 3

Compelled

I like shoes. I also like boots. I even like sandals and flip-flops. Because I do, I'm easily *attracted* to both brick and mortar as well as online shoe stores. (This is true, not a made-up story!)

The more special the shoe, the quicker I am to pick it up or rifle through an online catalog. In other words, a unique shoe is a pretty good way to engage me. So, what stores, or brands or styles *compel* me to buy a pair of shoes? None of them. Not a single one. I hope you're wondering why.

You *compel yourself; I don't compel you.*

When you realize you're standing at a fork in the road you have no option but to choose a single path. At the end of the day, you're compelled to choose what you choose because your choice is connected to your want.

Not my want, not somebody else's want, *your* want.

Here's a great tip I hope you'll try out. When crafting your conversation, create dialogue so that your audience is *in* the scene, not watching the scene. In doing so, the people you serve become a part of their own story, rather than a spectator of their story. This is how you help others come to realize they're actually standing at the fork in the road, not looking down the road at it.

So, how do we get to a place where we find ourselves wanting to choose?

My former office was a log cabin we had built and then moved onto the Indiana property we were living on at the time. I loved this space for its simplicity—one room with a lot of windows overlooking a serene pond surrounded by massive trees and a man-made waterfall at the far end of the pond. We had moved from Minnesota just one year earlier. Not knowing where I wanted to have my office, I had started out in a corner of our basement. Three teenagers at the time made for a less than stellar situation. I considered renting an office off the quaint brick-lined main street in Zionsville or simply renting space from Regus offices, a multi-level commercial office building catering to small business owners like me. Yet, I never pulled the trigger. I just couldn't get excited about a traditional office environment.

Then one Saturday morning while out on a three-hundred-mile joy ride on my Harley Davidson, I turned onto a road where there sat a number of log cabins, fully built and ready to be moved.

A light bulb went on!

That's it, I thought! I'll have a little log cabin built and moved onto the very back of our property and that will be my office. The rest is history. I moved into my new working space several months later. As I write this, I'm laughing out loud because I was *literally* on a road and, although my motorcycle wasn't actually at a fork in the road, my mind sure was. And, in that exact moment, I became compelled to make my choice. For me, the path I was on (officing in my basement) led me to the fork in the road: staying in my own little basement corner versus finding a space outside my home.

Please catch this next thought.

I wasn't compelled to get out of my basement until I saw myself choosing the other path—the log cabin. The other path (officing somewhere other than my basement) was not, in and of itself, in any way compelling. Then one day, when my office dilemma was far from my mind, I found myself at the fork making a rather easy decision. It was that compelling. To bring more depth to how this is such a significant part of crafting the client conversation, let's spend a little time better understanding the word *compel.*

In most dictionaries, *to compel* seems to have a rather negative connotation. Take a look at a few of the synonyms given: *to force, to drive, to make, to coerce.* That doesn't sound good. And when you throw up a few other phrases, including *to persuade, to convince* and *to coax*, one might quickly conclude that I've chosen the wrong word to describe this third piece of crafting the client conversation.

Choosing *to compel* is, however, very intentional and is perhaps one of the strongest differentiating aspects of my take on how so many people get the client conversation wrong.

The verbs above—to persuade, to convince, to coax— are often associated with sales training. *Persuade* seems like a natural sales word. After all, in sales, isn't it my job to convince you that what I have to offer is the missing link in your chain? I've sat through dozens, if not hundreds of training sessions, conferences and presentations over the past thirty-five-plus years where the purpose of the talk was to teach techniques of persuasion (*The Power of Persuasion*).

Now, I'm not about to throw the baby out with the bath water, it's just that persuasion isn't an effective standalone approach. *When your primary client conversation method is persuasion, you're likely to come across as pitching.*

Let's take the word *convince.* You may be surprised to hear me say during an actual client conversation, "My job isn't to convince you of anything." That's right. My job isn't to convince or to persuade you to do or not do something. My job is to help you see and understand what you're doing, then help you see and understand whether what you're doing is likely to get you the outcomes you desire, assuming all the variables you don't control go your way. In other words, if what you're doing and how you're doing it is getting you the outcomes you want, great! You will see, know and understand that what you're doing is what you *should* keep doing.

If, on the other hand, what you're doing is not getting you the outcomes you want (assuming all variables in life you don't control go your way) then, guess what? You will find yourself at the fork in the road, where I've found myself numerous times. And you'll be compelled to make a choice between continuing to do what you're doing (path 1) or choosing a completely different path that better aligns your decisions with the outcomes you desire (path 2).

Seeing yourself standing at the fork in the road reminds me of a saying I heard well over two decades ago. I don't recall who first shared the thought, but it goes like this:

"Until the pain of same is greater than the pain of change, you will not change."

You choose one path or the other. Standing at the fork in the road is not an option. The beauty of this word picture is that you cannot choose both paths.

I don't compel you to change. You compel yourself to change.

My role is to be a part of your journey, helping you see what you didn't know you didn't know.

Let's shift gears a bit and dive into another significant characteristic of this concept—that these two paths cannot be variations of one another. Rather, these two paths must be exclusive of one another. Different. Unique. Below are two lists.

List 1

- A horse is not a cow – yet both are animals
- A truck is not a bicycle – yet both are forms of transportation
- A pork chop is not a candy bar – yet both are considered food

Ask yourself, what is the context? There is no context related to "paths" or a "fork in the road". Therefore, when you are helping someone see themselves standing in the fork in road, you must build the context around the information you have to work with. Read through the next list.

List 2

- If you want to get milk from a farmer, you find one with cows.
- If you want to ride on a narrow, paved trail along the shoreline of Lake Superior, you ride a bicycle.
- If you want to hand out sweets to kids on Halloween, you buy a bag of candy.

See the incredible difference? See how the conversation suddenly turns from focusing on common information to creating a scenario built around their 'want'?

Using the phrase, "If you want _____, you _____."

- If you want milk from a farmer, you find a farmer with cows, not a farmer with horses.
- If you want to put a down payment on a house, you have to have access to money that is available for a down payment.
- If you want to retire someday, you need to have income that doesn't require you to work for it.

One of the most effective ways to make sure you are barking up the right tree is to write out an *If* statement. Look back on the three *If* statements above. These statements create clarity.

Remember, a fork in the road must provide two completely different alternatives.

Let's try another story to drive home the difference between compelling someone to action, as compared to being compelled to action yourself.

How are you sleeping?

Not well. You wake up day after day unrested, irritable, frustrated and tired. At least that's what your spouse and kids are telling you. You don't think anything is wrong, but you want your family to get off your back, so you agree to go to a sleep study institute to find out what may be keeping you up at night.

You travel to an overnight sleep study clinic where staff will monitor your sleep. Machines are hooked up to you. The bed and the room itself have various sensors and there's even a video camera that captures all the visual data. You fall asleep, toss and turn like most nights, and wake up feeling no different than if you had awakened in your own bed. You get dressed and wait in another room for a staff member to share the initial results with you. Fifteen minutes pass before the door opens and a friendly staff member enters the room.

> "How did you sleep last night?" she asks.
> "Fine, I guess. Didn't seem that different than at home."

"Okay, good," she says. "Do you feel unrested, irritable, frustrated or tired?"

"Not really. I feel like I usually feel," you reply, somewhat annoyed. "I'm here because my wife bugged me for so long that I wanted to prove to her everything is fine and that it's her issue, not mine."

"I have a bunch of data from the monitors and sensors, as well as some visual observations from the staff watching you sleeping last night. However, rather than start there, I'd like to show you a video that captures several moments of you sleeping last night. How does that sound to you?"

"Well sure," you say, with just a bit more annoyance in your voice. "You're the expert."

The video plays.

You see yourself trying to fall asleep, tossing and turning a bit until you finally clonk out. A few minutes later you see yourself lying flat on your back when your body suddenly goes eerily still. Your mouth is wide open and it appears that you're not breathing.

You remain silent and keep watching.

A few minutes later, the very same scene unfolds again. You see yourself lifeless. You cannot deny that what you see happening happened just moments before.

Then you see it happen a third time.

"Wow," you mumble.

You watch yourself stop breathing a fourth time, but this time you appear to gag before somehow rolling over onto your side. You just saw yourself jump start your own breathing as your body appeared to labor for a moment.

"What do I need to do so this doesn't happen again?" you ask the young woman, this time with urgency in your voice.

You find yourself at the fork in the road and are compelled to take action in an instant. There are no statistics from the sensors and monitors, no dialogue about the risks and potential consequences of living with sleep apnea. You simply saw yourself not breathing for an extended period of time. Not once, not twice, not three times, but four. And you know, even without seeing proof, there were more times.

This is why *compel* is so powerful a word with respect to the client conversation. No persuasion, no convincing, no coaxing. In a matter of minutes, you saw what others believed to be true but didn't have the proof to show you. You agreed to do the sleep study to get your family off your back, but you now realize their nagging may have just saved your life.

Compelling you to action, immediate action, begins with helping you see, perhaps for the first time in your life, that what you thought was the right way to get what you wanted won't, in fact, get you what you want.

You believe—again, perhaps for the first time in your life—there is no way for you to get what you want if you keep doing what you're doing. You instantly realize you need help.

You are given an opportunity to choose to get help or not get help. If you choose to get help you want to believe the help is real and it's what it takes to get you closer to the outcome you want. You are compelled to action when you first come to grips with the reality and truth of your existing world. Yes, your existing world!

Seeing and believing the shortcomings of your present reality is crucial in compelling yourself to action.

You can't see your own blind spots. If you could see them, they wouldn't be called blind spots. Crafting conversations around the blind spots of the people you serve is oftentimes how they find themselves standing in the fork in the road. And when they see themselves standing in the fork in the road, they compel themselves to action.

Technical skill is mastery of complexity, while creativity is mastery of simplicity.

Sir Erik Christopher Zeewan

Chapter 4

Doubly Good

What can Nancy A. Noel hold over the head of Pablo Picasso? For one thing, her poster reproductions outsold his in the 1990s.

Picasso (1881-1973) is arguably one of the greatest artists of the past one thousand years. His name alone speaks volumes. Nancy A. Noel (1945-2020) is one of the most accomplished artists you've likely never heard of. She is known here in Indiana because she lived her life just down the road from where I live. Her gallery in a beautiful historic building was a bona fide tourist attraction until she closed it down a few years ago. Walking through to see her work was breathtaking.

Picasso and Noel are part of a very small group of artists considered to be technically superior in their ability to paint precise, lifelike people, animals, structures, as well as earthly and heavenly scenes. Yet both are also known for their ability to evoke deep, moving emotion from admirers of their work. Perhaps the smallest group of artists of all—an extraordinarily small group—includes those who are both superior in technical skill and in their ability to elicit an unmatched breadth and depth of emotion from those experiencing their work. Being doubly good—both a great technician and an artist capturing moving emotion—is a feat very few accomplish.

So, hopefully you are asking yourself, Huh? How do Picasso and Nancy Noel fit into a book on conversational selling? Let me share with you.

First, a question for you, my fellow salesperson: How do people view you in your work with them? Do they see you as someone who knows their stuff, but doesn't know how to connect well emotionally?

"Great doctor, terrible bedside manner!"

Do they see you as a great person to hang with but someone who lacks confidence in their ability to put the technical pieces together?

"What a great guy. Just not sure he knows what he's doing."

Or do they see you as part of an extraordinarily small group of practitioners with both superior technical and emotional abilities?

"Wow! She blows me away! I feel amazing with her in our corner! And does she ever know how all this works! We're so fortunate to have been introduced to this wonderful lady!"

Most of you will agree that there's an artistic side as well as a technical side to many things in life. The few who master their craft tend to be doubly good—on both the artistic side and the technical side of their craft. In the next few pages you will see how learning to have meaningful conversations is one of those areas where you want to be doubly good.

PART 1

Let's begin with a look at the Technical pieces of a meaningful conversation, starting with a five-part technical framework I've created called TIDADS.

TIDADS

- T – choosing a big picture TOPIC
- I – having one leading IDEA throughout each unique conversation
- DA – knowing the DESIRED ACTION you want the person you are interacting with to want to want to take prior to y'all having conversation together

- D – building the DIALOGUE – including specific words and phrases to use, as well as words and phrases not to use
- S – preparing the STUFF – stories, imagery, illustrations, metaphors, examples and props are among the types of resources you will imbed into your conversation

All effective conversations in the sales environment have an opening, a closing, and an in-between. I am making an assumption that these three elements are broadly accepted by most readers. Therefore, our focus is on the technical framework of a conversation, with the focus on helping others DO something, BUY something, OWN something, CHANGE something, IMPROVE something, or MOVE ON from something. Let's break down TIDADS a bit more by using an example from the world of personal finance.

T is for TOPIC

Topics are aplenty in the personal financial realm, including retirement, borrowing money, investing, college, financial planning, risk management, and buying a house, among others.

- Let's choose RETIREMENT as our TOPIC.

I is for the leading IDEA

What are some possible leading IDEAS inside the

TOPIC of RETIREMENT? How about saving for retirement, planning for retirement, living in retirement someday, living in retirement now, creating income in retirement, among others?

Let's choose LIVING IN RETIREMENT SOMEDAY as our leading IDEA.

DA is for DESIRED ACTION

So, we are moving from the TOPIC of RETIREMENT to the leading IDEA of LIVING IN RETIREMENT SOMEDAY, to now identifying the DESIRED ACTION I want you to want to take as a result of our upcoming interaction.

This is where it gets fun.

If you and I have never met, yet are connecting today over a cup of coffee, would it be unreasonable for me to assume you will move all of your financial decisions over to my firm because we are sharing 20 minutes together over a cup of coffee? Yes! That would be a ridiculous expectation on my part.

So, what do I WANT you to want to do as result of our getting together for 20 minutes or so over a cup of coffee? I want you to desire to have another conversation. That is the outcome I really do want. That's it.

- Let's agree then that the DESIRED ACTION I want

you to take as a result of this one interaction is for you to desire and agree to another conversation.

You may be asking, why did you choose LIVING IN RETIREMENT SOMEDAY as the leading IDEA and not PLANNING FOR RETIREMENT or CREATING INCOME IN RETIREMENT or some other IDEA that seems to be more common in this TOPIC space today?

For one, LIVING IN RETIREMENT SOMEDAY is something most people actually want. In the nearly 25 years I have been in the financial services industry, I have yet to find a single person who actually WANTS SAVING FOR RETIREMENT or PREPARING FOR RETIREMENT. Nope! The people we serve don't want saving or preparing—they want living.

You and I are chatting over a cup of coffee for the very first time, so it seems quite reasonable for me to want you to desire something simple and non-threatening. Do you agree that wanting you to desire to have another conversation fits the simple and non-threatening category? In other words, the action I want you to take as a result of our first conversation is to have another conversation. That's it. And I want you to want this.

Now, before you throw this book away, the DESIRED ACTION each time you interact with someone is not simply to have another conversation. Absolutely not! You want the person you are serving to take different desired action steps as a result of different conversations you will walk them through.

Below is a list of other DESIRED ACTIONS within the TOPIC of RETIREMENT ? How about:

- Saving for retirement
- Planning for retirement
- Living in retirement someday
- Living in retirement now
- Creating income in retirement

Frankly, one of the secrets to the TIDADS technique is to build out a list of actions—actual steps—to continue or to begin taking now. The key to identifying specific DESIRED ACTIONS is to put them in proper sequence. It's not a whole lot different than putting together a piece of furniture that has 12 assembly steps; performed in the wrong order, you can end up standing a brand-new bookshelf up against the wall without any shelves for your books to rest on.

D is for DIALOGUE

Another of the secrets to this technique is to design your dialogue by starting with the DESIRED ACTION you want the other person to take as a result of your interaction.

I'm serious.

Start with the END in mind. Start with the DESIRED ACTION.

If you don't know what you want the person you are having a conversation with to do as a result of your interaction, it's pretty safe to say they won't have a clue either.

In collaboration with Norm Trainor and Dr. Keita Demming at The Covenant Group, I have delivered a series of workshops built to take the content of this book deeper with those who see the potential of these principles and techniques to help those you are serving get what they want, as well as help you get what you want. If you want to increase your revenue and also positively enhance the feel and flow of your conversations with others, keep reading. Afterall, this book is focused on providing a framework, along with an overview of several time-tested and proven conversation techniques.

Every word chosen has been selected with great care and thought. Let me explain.
Words really do matter. If you're like me, there are times I use words that are close, but not quite right. Words that are descript, but not warm and inviting. Words that are warm and inviting, but don't really say anything.

I absolutely love the definition of dialogue at yourdictionary.com: dialogue is conversation. How cool is that? Dialogue is a conversation.

Too many people in the sales environment treat DIALOGUE as a free-flow exchange with few, if any guardrails around that exchange. A free-for-all is not a desirable picture of DIALOGUE in conversational selling. Rather, DIALOGUE is intended to be a structured conversation. As you continue to turn the pages, you will come across a deeper dive into techniques to structure dialogue without feeling like you're delivering a canned presentation.

S is for STUFF

Okay Dean, STUFF? Really? That's the best word you got? Perhaps you were thinking this. If so, let's start with a quick thought on why the word STUFF fits here. STUFF includes everything, even the kitchen sink. Stories. Images. Sketches. Word pictures. Diagrams. Charts. Metaphors. Pauses. Props. Emotions. Pacing. Anything that helps bring a story to life.

You, my friend, will have effectively started using the TIDADS technique when you have:

- Your TOPIC
- Your clearly defined leading IDEA
- Your crystal clear DESIRED ACTION
- Your structured DIALOGUE
- Your STUFF woven and imbedded into your dialogue

I look forward to you sharing how using TIDADS has positively influenced your conversations and hearing how the TIDADS framework is impacting your results! Text me at 317-659-3020.

PART 2

Now let's look at the key Artistic pieces that create meaningful conversation, starting with a simple thought to set context. Conversational selling is about creating an amazing experience for the person you are conversing with, as well as for you.

An amazing experience?

Remember the story of my uncle Glen at the beginning of this book? Like all the personal stories in this book, there is something special for me when I think back to moments so long ago. Great memories always seem to be tied to great experiences.

How about you? Think about a time where you had a conversation and the experience was memorable in all the best ways.

- How old were you?
- Where were you?
- Who else was there?
- What was happening?
- Why does it come to mind now?
- How is this experience memorable?

Back a very long time ago I was an actor in high school. So, I want us to use live theater as the backdrop for developing the artistic side of having conversations in a selling context.

Blocking the Set

"In theat[er], blocking is the precise staging of actors to facilitate the performance of a play, ballet, film or opera."[2] Below is more of what Wikipedia has to say about blocking. While you read, have in your mind's eye the visual of sitting with a prospective client over a cup of coffee. In other words, read through the description, but instead of seeing a play or ballet performance, imagine watching all this happen in the setting of conversational selling. Wikipedia continues:

> There are also *artistic reasons* why blocking can be crucial. Through careful use of positioning on the stage, a director or performer can establish or change the significance of a scene. Different artistic principles can inform blocking, including minimalism and naturalism.

Imagine a live set with actors and props and lighting and positioning and entrances and exits and often transitions and—well, you likely get the point.

Do you pay attention to how you can set the stage for a more meaningful conversation?

- Where you have conversations.
- Where you sit in a coffee shop or restaurant.
- Where you sit at a kitchen or board room table.
- Whether you sit or stand during a live web-based video conversation.

---

[2] https://en.wikipedia.org/wiki/Blocking_(stage)

- When you arrive.
- When they arrive.
- When you leave.
- When they leave.
- Which direction you face.
- Which direction they face.
- Where you place your hands.
- The gestures you use, don't use or overuse.
- The language the other person uses and how you could better match their style.
- How long you make small talk at the start of your conversation.
- How long and how often you pause during your conversation.
- How fast or slow your pace is throughout your conversation.
- How you infuse word pictures related to their world into your conversation.
- What words to avoid during your conversation.
- How you pick up on new words to use as your conversation goes along.
- How your audience—your client or prospective client—responds to you.
- How you adjust your pace, your word pictures, your words and phrases throughout your conversation.

When you design your conversations ahead of time, you find the freedom to improvise, when appropriate, so the conversation is warm, genuine, and laced with authentic natural expressions.

Think about a live play you have attended in the past. Perhaps you yourself even performed back in the day. Imagine a troupe of actors taking the stage opening night at the Orpheum Theatre! You are center stage, twelve rows back. Perfect seats. The show being performed is one of your absolute favorites. Me, I'm envisioning *Les Misérables.* Now, imagine the lights go down, the curtains go up and Scene One begins.

There's a pause. A long pause. A very long pause. Then you hear a whisper, just loud enough for the entire theater to hear coming from stage left. You hear faintly, "Steve, who goes out first, you or me?" Perhaps this would be cute if you are envisioning a middle school play. However, if you paid good money for your center seats in Row 12, my guess is you wouldn't be laughing. You would likely be appalled, upset or downright ticked off.

Early in my own career, I failed to recognize the importance of all the nuances of the selling environment. Once I recognized that the selling experience is simply wrapped up in a series of conversations, my perspective changed dramatically.

Blocking the play *Les Misérables* is not just for the benefit of the actors. I contend that the ultimate purpose of blocking is for the audience's benefit. Afterall, a lead or supporting actor's role is to create a memorable experience for the audience. And when the actor gives the audience what they want, the actor gets what he or she wants.

It's really no different in conversational selling.

Look back at the Wikipedia entry to read the following again:

> There are also *artistic reasons* why blocking can be crucial. Through careful use of positioning on the stage, a director or performer can establish or change the significance of a scene. Different artistic principles can inform blocking, including minimalism and naturalism.

The artistic elements of conversational selling include your personality, your style, your level of energy, your expressions, your timing, your believability—ultimately, YOU! Without proper blocking of your conversational selling interactions, you greatly limit your freedom to interact well with your audience. In other words, having clarity on the technical aspects of conversational selling gives you the freedom to bring your artistic abilities front and center.

Please don't underestimate the power of performance. At the same time, don't disregard the role the technical pieces play. When you are doubly good—technically sound and artistically gifted—you greatly enhance the experiences you create and increase your results.

To get what you want help others get what they want.

Zig Ziglar

Chapter 5

You, not me!

Over the past fifteen years I have developed a unique friendship with Verlyn Fast, a successful farmer and entrepreneur from my hometown of Mountain Lake, Minnesota. We both love riding our Harley Davidson motorcycles long distances across the United States. Verlyn comes to mind when I think about someone who focuses on the other person.

Verlyn is always quick to bring the conversation back around to whoever he's visiting with. He's genuinely interested in what you think, what you believe, why you do what you do and why you don't do what you don't do. To say Verlyn and I have shared some deep, personal conversations about life is an understatement. I could not have predicted over fifteen years ago that one of my closest friends and confidants would one day be my buddy Verlyn. I'm convinced much of our ongoing friendship is built around dialogue, where we each focus on the other. It feels a lot like playing tennis, a game we both picked up a couple of years ago. A good rally is all about keeping the ball in play for as long as possible by hitting it back over the net to the other guy.

That's how it is with conversations.

- You find yourself in great conversations when you focus on the other person.
- You find yourself ducking sales pitches when you focus on the other person.
- You find yourself avoiding long presentations and boring monologues when you focus on the other person.
- You find yourself learning meaningful insights when you focus on the other person.
- You find yourself hearing what they actually mean, when you focus on the other person.
- You find yourself energized when you focus on the other person.
- You find yourself helping others when you focus on the other person.
- You find yourself satisfied when you focus on the other person.

Simply put, when you focus on the other person, you give yourself a great chance to be in conversation with them. Sounds easy, right? Not exactly!

In the sales environment, I have found that conversations are not the norm. Pitches are the norm. Yet, after decades of experience, I have become convinced that crafting the client conversation is one of the most fundamental ingredients for a meaningful and successful career in sales. Crafting the client conversation isn't simple, nor is it complicated. It is, instead, complex. And, as Keita Demming at The Covenant Group has taught me, anything complex can be simplified through the use of straightforward rules, guidelines and principles. This makes crafting the client conversation formulaic.

If you think about it, there are two primary ways in which you can approach an interaction with another person. The first is making it about me, the second is making it about them. The first way (all about me) ignores the notion of attracting the other person into a conversation. When you focus on the other person first, however, you create a gateway for *attracting* them into a conversation about a leading idea that turns out to really matter to them.

The interplay of words and expressions must be genuine and authentic, so they feel and believe the conversation is about them. It's remarkable how someone is compelled to take action that helps them get what they want when they see that my motivation is simply to help them get what they want. It all starts by attracting them into meaningful, you-focused conversation.

You-focused conversations are designed to help the other person take steps naturally—the kind of steps they are not sure how to take—to get where they want to be. Me-focused conversations really aren't conversations at all. Me-focused interactions end up feeling like a sales pitch because the pitchman is pitching the benefits of his me-focused deal.

So, why does this matter at all?

For starters, many industries, professions and careers have largely earned their reputations from being me-focused. When you think of the following professions do you think of them as being me-focused or you-focused?

- Car salesman
- Insurance Agent
- Cell phone representative
- Door-to-Door salesperson
- Multi-level marketing representative

You likely agree that each of these careers is stereotypically me-focused. Pushy, salesy, over-bearing, hard-selling, and won't-take-no-for-an-answer too often accurately describe these me-focused players. When pressed for a useful and accurate description, most people label each of these me-focused people a salesperson. When you sit with a person who has a salesperson label you often end up feeling pitched. And, if you're like me, you don't like being pitched to.

Let's bring this to the industry I've been a part of since 1998, financial services. There are typically two ways in which you will connect with someone in the financial services world:

1. You may be seeking help. When you seek help, you may want advice, direction, or simply desire clarity about some financial topic impacting your life.

2. You may not be actively seeking help. You nonetheless respond to a call, email, or personal introduction from a friend and agree to give the financial professional a bit of your time.

Whether you are seeking help from others or someone is reaching out first to offer help, you likely are not wanting to get together just to experience the feeling of being pitched.

We're far more informal in the way we communicate today than perhaps at any time in history. What's different today is how people have grown to rely heavily on alternate forms of communication, most of which didn't exist until the early 2000s. Texting, social forums, blogs, instant messaging, directed emails, and even present-day social media channels like *LinkedIn* and *Twitter* have revolutionized the way in which people receive information, advice and direction.

To take it one step further, two types of people are reading this book:

- One remembers using rotary dial phones, leaving messages on answering machines or asking a secretary, personal assistant, co-worker, spouse or even a child answering the phone at home if they would jot down a note.
- The second type of person doesn't remember these things at all!

Take texting. Some estimates suggest that six billion text messages are sent each day. *Six billion!* A text typically consists of a few words or letters. Y*o. K. Sup. LOL. U git the pt.* A single text is rarely more than thirty words. *(Do some instant research: Check out your last twenty texts and count the number of words in each. Text me at 317-659-3020 to let me know what you find out.)*

The purpose of a text is most often to quickly communicate a brief and specific message to the recipient. Like you, I have been on both the sending and receiving end of text messages gone wrong. There's nothing wrong with text messaging. It's just that a text message can lack context that helps people fill in the emotional cracks that are meant to complement words. Yet, people make huge decisions from text messages all the time.

When you consider the widespread use and acceptance of social media channels along with the internet, it should come as no surprise that many choose to make life-altering financial decisions using the framework they rely on for finding a restaurant, planning a vacation or buying a new vacuum cleaner. It's remarkable the number of people today who text a message or reach out through social media, never thinking to pick up the phone to call. There is nothing inherently wrong with any of these communication formats. However, what has gone wrong is how four (soon to be five) generations seem to struggle with face-to-face conversation. Interaction has become more an exercise of your digits than your vocal cords.

Of course, you may be reading this and thinking, but Dean, you can insert emojis to create the emotion you want to create! True. But not true. Emoji's and GIF's most definitely point to emotions. But do they create emotional connections? That's like saying a torch lighter is a fire. A torch lighter starts a fire, but to call it a fire is a stretch. So too is the use of all the add-on's that come with the digital devices overtaking our world today. I love emoji's and GIF's, but I use them as I do punctuation in a letter.

Frankly, one of my hopes is for you to become compelled to use the conversational techniques we teach you throughout this book. Deep, enriching, emotionally engaging, live conversation is becoming a lost art, a lost practice, a lost part of our culture. Healthy conversation is dying. Now, after several decades of helping people, I continue to hone my technical skills and artistic abilities to hold meaningful conversations with people.

Remember, this book is about conversational selling: helping you to attract and engage others so that they compel themselves to take action that helps them get what they want. Because of my years of experience in the financial services world, this book uses examples from the financial services industry. But, as an entrepreneur I know *these techniques are transferrable to any industry where relationships matter.* And these guidelines, principles and techniques transfer and apply in most contexts. This includes both your professional and personal life, no matter if the communication is formal or informal, written or oral, or even non-verbal.

Let's switch gears and begin breaking down common challenges people in the sales environment face in their work with others.

A sunrise is God's way of saying, "Let's Start Again."

Todd Stocker

Chapter 6

Ready! Set! Go!

Wilbur Shaw is given credit for being the first to say, "Gentlemen, start your engines!" before the start of the 1953 Indianapolis 500 race. Every year since, some variation of this famous statement has been used, including today's standard call, "Drivers, start your engines!" All the pomp and circumstance is soon in the rear-view mirrors of the drivers, as they fire their engines and begin to circle the famous 2.5 mile track in the heart of Speedway, Indiana to compete in the 500 mile race.

So, how do you start your conversations?

I'm serious. What words do you use to engage others in conversations? After all, either there is a clear starting point or there is not.

Drivers, start your engines!
Once upon a time,
Ready! Set! Go!

Each one of these expressions is likely familiar to you. These phrases speak to all of us more profoundly than we may at first think. We will use *Ready! Set! Go!* to help shape our next section and define how you may want to start every conversation.

PART 1: Ready!

Any conversation in the sales world should be clearly defined by two distinct phases:

> Phase 1 – Small Talk
> Phase 2 – Big Talk

You will find an incredibly simple way to move from small talk to big talk. You simply blurt out the following nine words to move into the big talk:

> "Hey Jerry, do you mind if we jump in?"

Or you could say:

> "Jerry, are you ready to stop this small talk and get into the big talk?"

Repeat those words:

"Jerry, are you ready to stop this small talk and get into the big talk?"

It sounds kind of weird to the ear. You would probably never say those words. I wouldn't. Now say the following aloud to yourself.

"Hey Jerry, do you mind if we jump in?"

Doesn't really sound weird, does it? These nine words simply communicate that you are wanting permission to move from meaningful small talk to the purpose you agreed to get together—the big talk.

Let's back up a couple of minutes or so, prior to these nine words coming out of your mouth. Let's set the scene. If Jerry and I are getting together at a coffee shop at 9 a.m., I arrive at the coffee shop a good ten minutes early to scope out the best table. I want to ensure that I sit facing the room and Jerry's view will be of the wall behind me. Less distraction. We grab our coffees when they're ready and seat ourselves at the table right around 9 a.m. We share meaningful small talk for a couple of minutes, along the lines of the following:

- "So, how was your drive over to the coffee shop today?"
- "Larry, our mutual friend, mentioned y'all

attended the University of Minnesota. Me too!"
- "I hear you have quite the whistling talent...so says Larry!"

Then, after just enough time to make a human connection, hopefully laced with a good chuckle or two, you utter the nine words you use before every conversation you have.

"Hey Jerry, do you mind if we jump in?"

And the conversation begins.

By the way, if you are having a virtual coffee the first time you get together, you simply jump on a video-conferencing app and start with similar small talk.

Yes, you were having conversation about some common connection that creates a human bond, but without these nine-words, you will struggle to clearly move into the conversation you're there to share together. The beauty of the nine-word question is that it expresses confidence, purpose, and respect for their time, as well as your own. And you fulfill a second critical element of crafting a successful client conversation—*gaining permission to proceed.*

When you focus on the other person (the first critical element) and gain or regain permission to proceed (the second critical element), you endear yourself to the person you are with. You must mean it. You must truly want to put them before you; if not, it will all backfire on you.

PART 2: Set!

Have you ever suddenly found yourself on a page different from the one the person you are interacting with is on? Or can you think of a time where you and this other person agreed to get together on some basis, and then when you got together it dawned on you part-way through the conversation that the other person clearly didn't recall why you were getting together?

Let's fix this awkwardness right now.

After you have been given permission to jump in, you want to ensure that you are set on what the big talk is focused on. Here is the question to ask every time. Yes, every time!

> "Before we jump in, what are you expecting today?"

What? Really? Isn't this dangerous, Dean? Whoa, Dean, won't I lose control if I give them an opportunity to redirect the conversation? Nope, quite the opposite. You may be mixing up questions. The nine-word question above is *not* the same as asking:

- What do you want to talk about today?
- What's on your mind?
- Do you want to talk about how we help people?

No, these are all terrible questions to ask. Why are these terrible questions to ask, Dean? Because these questions leave the door open for you to lose control of the direction of the dialogue. When you first reach out to someone, you *must* establish an expectation of getting together and, frankly, you must do so each time thereafter. When you conclude a conversation with a clear description and understanding of why you are getting back together, the prospective client or client has given you permission to re-establish the expectation of getting together.

It's simple.

We will come back to *Part 2: Set!* for some additional insight after first walking through *Part 3: Go!*

PART 3: Go!

Go! comes into play the very first time you get together with a *prospective* client. This first interaction is different than any other conversation you will ever have with the person you are interacting with. You are likely familiar with the notion of first impressions. Go! is a reference to where your prospective client wants to ultimately go. You may think of this part as the hole they want to drill out. You will read a story about the hole in Chapter 9. The drill is a point-blank question you ask. In our work with those we serve, our point-blank question is:

"I'm curious, do you want to retire someday?"

Why would you ask such a question? And what makes it a point-blank question?

You ask the question because you want to know *their* want. What do they want? What do they ultimately want? Not knowing the response to the point-blank question puts you into a black hole. The black hole is the reality that you really don't know where they want to go.

The people we enjoy helping want to retire someday and live a life they have dreamed of living without worry and fear. Hearing them respond to this question helps us help them.

Help them how, Dean?

Help them realize that every decision during their working years affects their ability to retire and live the life they have dreamed of living without worry and fear. Calling this out within the first few minutes of connecting with someone for the first time suddenly makes your conversation have incredible focus on something *they* want!

Now, you may be in a different segment of the financial services world or you may be in some other industry altogether. So, you must ask yourself, what do the ideal clients I seek to help WANT? Really, really want. Once you are clear on their ultimate want, only then can you write out your point-blank *Go! question.* Remember, the point-blank question is one that must cut to the ULTIMATE WANT of the people you serve.

You once again may put this off as overly simplistic. This one question alone has the potential to transform your world, regardless of the industry you are in.

Part 2 – Set! BONUS MATERIAL

"Before we jump in, what are you expecting today?"

We established a moment ago that this is the question you ask to re-establish the focus of your conversation—focusing on the Big Talk. In order to frame the technique, we are going to walk through the scripted dialogue that takes place prior to your asking this question. (NOTE: the suggested telephone script below includes multiple common objections. Typically, you will not receive all of these objections from one person. However, it is easiest to share with you in succession the common natural push-backs shared by most people.)

THE SET-UP:

A mutual acquaintance introduces you and your prospective client to one another, oftentimes in an email introduction.

You telephone the prospective client, saying something like the following:

"Hi Jerry, this is Dean Harder. Our mutual friend Larry introduced us to one another the other day via email. Do you have a moment?"

"Sure."

"Jerry, I'd love to get together over a cup of coffee—either in person or virtually—in the next few weeks, for twenty to thirty minutes to learn more about your world, as well as show you how we help people. I'm wondering what your work hours are, what time you get rolling in the morning?"

"I get into the office around seven a.m. most mornings."

"Great Jerry. How about connecting at ten a.m. either Tuesday or Thursday next week at the neighborhood coffee shop near your office. Or, if you want to do a virtual cup instead, we can do that too. What is good for you?"

"Thursday works fine for me next week at ten a.m. at the coffee shop down the street from my office."

"Great Jerry. Sounds good. By the way, Jane Perkins from our office will touch base the day before, simply to make sure you and I are both good to go. Let either one of us know if something comes up in the meantime and we'll simply find another spot. We'll do the same if something surprises our schedule. Cool with you, Jerry?"

"Works for me Dean. Thanks."

"Great. Be well. See you next week, Jerry."

COMMON OBJECTIONS

#1: "What's this about, Dean?"

"Glad you asked, Jerry. That's why I'd love to get together for twenty to thirty minutes, to actually show you how we help people. So, what time do you get rolling in the morning?"

#2: "If this is about financial stuff, I'm pretty well set. I wouldn't want to waste your time, Dean."

"That's alright, Jerry, I have no reason to believe you and I should have a business relationship. I simply want to show you how we help people, then you and I can decide if there is any reason to chat further. So, how 'bout we catch a virtual cup of coffee either next week or the following for twenty minutes or so?"

#3: "Well, I'd really like to Dean, but I'm awfully busy the next couple of weeks."

"That's cool, Jerry. Most of the people we share time with are busy people. That's why I only want to grab twenty minutes or so of time together. How 'bout we look a month out? What does your life look like then?

"Sure Dean. I can do it after I get through this crazy time. Let's shoot for a virtual cup of coffee Tuesday at ten a.m. three weeks out."

"Great, Jerry, thanks. See you then."

It is worth noting that this phone call is extremely typical with 95% of the conversation being a standardized script and 5% being customized. So, with this phone script deeply seeded in your mind, you have the secret as to why we would ask, "Before we jump in, what are you expecting today?" Let's see how this sequence of scripted dialogue positions you to gain agreement on something you have already agreed to.

In the years I've been using this simple 9-question technique, there have only been two types of responses; not three, not four, not five. *Just two*. The first response we'll call the right response, the second we'll call the wrong response.

Here's the question one more time:

"Before we jump in, what were you expecting today?"

The right response, seldom actually spoken is:

"You mentioned on the phone that you wanted to show me how you help people. Is that right?"

"Yep!"

That's the right response because when we agreed on a time to get together for 20-30 minute for an in-person or virtual cup of coffee, we also agreed to connect on the basis of my showing you how we help people. For now, you should conclude you will use the nine-word question only because you know there's only *one* right answer. Remember, *you* asked to get together and, as long as you said, "to show you how we help people" your question is more than appropriate—and absolutely critical, I might add!

The wrong response is any response other than the one expressed above.

When you invite someone to have a conversation and they have agreed to get together on the basis of what you expressed, you have earned the right to confirm the expectation when you get together. If you don't set and then re-set the expectation, well, anything goes. Below are a few typical *wrong* responses.

- I don't have any expectations.
- I imagine you want to sell me something.
- I'm guessing you have a pitch to give me.

- I suppose this is about what you sell.
- I think you're an advisor of some kind and want me to be your client.

Because you set an expectation prior to getting together you can engage on your terms—terms they have already agreed to. Perhaps you are now wondering how to respond when they respond the *wrong way*? Here you go:

"Well, as you may recall, when we chatted on the phone, I mentioned that I'd love to get together to simply show you how we help people. You alright if you and me chat about that?"

"Sure."

The response is "Sure." Why wouldn't it be? Perhaps this is one of the biggest differences between attracting someone into a conversation as compared to trying to immediately engage them in conversation. Let's look in a moment at some definitions to help you see the subtleties of these differences even more. For now, take note that you have relied on two 9-word questions to kick off every conversation:

Your *Ready!* question: "Hey Jerry, do you mind if we jump in?"

Your *Set!* Question: "Before we jump in, what are you expecting today?"

Pitchers and Conversationalists

Salespeople fall into two groups: *pitchers* and *conversationalists.* Pitchers tend to focus on the *what,* while conversationalists focus on the *want.*

Back in 1987, I signed up for an internship with a well-known life insurance company. The training was excellent. Excellent in that I really learned *what* we did. Looking back, however, I never learned the *why* behind the *what.* Over the course of six months I sold two life insurance policies, one to a friend and one to myself. I had several meetings with prospective buyers, so it's not that I didn't have anyone to talk to. But oh, what a failure of an internship it was on so many fronts! Yet that miserable experience, in part, is what set me on a course to mastering the art of conversation in the sales environment.

Fast forward from that experience to when I was re-introduced to the industry in 1998. I had sworn to myself back in '87 that I would never, ever get back into financial services, let alone the life insurance industry. But never say never.

This time something was very different. Ron Harder, a shirttail relative I had known since I was knee-high to a grasshopper, approached me after hearing I was leaving the family farm to do something else with my life. He came to our home and engaged Jackie and me in a unique way. He used the first twenty of our forty-five minutes together demonstrating to Jackie and me how an initial conversation goes with a prospective client. He used the remaining time to give an overview of the career opportunity.

Back to those first twenty minutes. Immediately, there was a feeling during those first twenty minutes that was completely different when compared to the ninety-minute first meeting I had learned to deliver during my pathetic internship about ten years earlier. In a matter of twenty minutes—through the use of a very simple, yet extraordinarily powerful system dubbed the Cotton System, designed, developed and trained by Wayne Cotton—I went from being a person who desperately wanted people to know how much I knew, to someone who wanted people to see and believe I was there to help them get what they wanted.

One of the biggest take-aways for me as I launched into a new career in '98 was my belief that a financial professional's responsibility—my responsibility—starts with helping a person, a couple, a family, a business, a non-profit or some other unique entity get what they want, something that matters to them. Look back to the beginning of this section and note the words I used to describe my internship, and how they differ from my description of my now long-time career.

I have come to realize that most people don't fully understand and appreciate the attraction phase of the client relationship. For years, I saw no differences between the *Attract* and *Engage* phases of the client conversation. The differences seemed more semantic than actual. So let's take an even deeper look and see why we want to differentiate the two phases of a conversation.

In conversational selling, the phrase to *have a liking for or interest in something* is a great description of the word *attract*, while *to participate or become involved* fits well for the word *engage*. While some dictionaries suggest that attract and engage are synonymous, the two words have distinctly different meanings in the context of conversational selling. Notice how *attract* includes the notion of having a liking for or interest in something. This can be spoken or unspoken. It can be known or unknown. And there's no commitment; it's merely about curiosity or interest.

I've long been attracted to the idea of being a private pilot. Yet not once have I ever engaged a single person in a conversation about what a first step might be in pursuing an interest I've had most of my adult life. I'm attracted to the idea of flying a small airplane, yet I've never, ever engaged in doing so.

In researching for this book, I didn't come across any material that takes the time to distinguish between *attract* and *engage* in the way I have come to recognize is essential in conversational selling. In fact, when researching the word *attract* within the sales environment, I found that *attract* is almost always used in the framework of marketing. In other words, *attracting people to have conversations* is used synonymously with *marketing to prospective clients.* Our work, particularly over the past fifteen years, strongly suggests that this element of attraction is more than just another word for marketing. My work with The Covenant Group has helped me understand that attracting is critical in the client conversation framework.

As a kid, my Grandma Hase made the greatest caramel rolls on the planet, while my Grandma Harder made the most amazing fresh loaves of bread. Grandma Harder also made Zwieback (commonly pronounced *tway-bach*), a Mennonite specialty. It's a yeast bread roll formed from two pieces of dough that are typically pulled apart when eaten. Oh my, you have no idea what you are missing if you've never had the real deal! The recipe for Zwieback calls for:

2 cups milk
¾ cup butter or lard
2 tbsp. yeast
3 cups flour
2 ½ tsp. salt

Imagine what these melt-in-your-mouth buns would look and taste like if you left out the yeast. (Who needs two tablespoons of yeast when you have three cups of flour?) Let's call the attraction phase the yeast and the flour the engagement phase. Yeast makes the flour mixture rise and that sounds to me a lot like attraction making engagement rise. Let's look at another example in an effort to distinguish attraction from engagement.

Fishing

- Scene 1: A fish sees a lure in the water.
- Scene 2: The fish begins to swim around the lure taking a closer look.
- Scene 3: The fish swims up close even briefly bumping the lure.
- Scene 4: The fish opens its mouth and takes the lure in.
- Scene 5: The fisherman responds.

Let's look at these scenes through the lenses of attraction and engagement.

- Scene 1: fish sees lure (*attracting*)
- Scene 2: fish takes a closer look (*attracted*)
- Scene 3: fish bumps lure (*transitioning*)
- Scene 4: fish goes for lure (*engaging*)
- Scene 5: fisherman responds. (*engaged*)

What responses does the fisherman consider?

1. Doesn't even notice the fish bumps his lure.
2. Do nothing and wait.
3. Tug gently on the line.
4. Yank the line quick and hard.

Many of you have fished at least once in your life. If you haven't, you've likely watched someone else fish. Setting the hook in the mouth of the fish is a pivotal moment—yes, moment—in the art of fishing. Setting the hook also has a technical aspect to it, so would say my cousin Jon Eric Hase, one of the best fishermen I know in Minnesota. Yes, setting the hook requires both technical and artistic ability. This too is the point of attracting and engaging those you wish to serve into meaningful client conversations. *You attract people into your world by focusing on their world*, so that they want to engage in further dialogue that brings your two worlds together. Too often we apologize in the sales arena for suggesting there's a hook you put in front of your clients. If you're in the business of feeding fish, drop worms in the water. If you want to catch fish, learn how to bait your hook, cast, reel and bring in your fish.

Please don't lose sight of the critical framework we've already laid out: *we're in the business of helping people get what they want!*

Imagine walking into your friend's backyard only to see him fly-fishing in his swimming pool. He may think he's fishing, but without any fish in the pool, he's no more fishing than I am while sitting in one of his poolside chairs. People often *think* the decisions they are making will get them what they want. But, like my buddy fishing in his fishless pool, his focus is on the wrong thing (unless you're watching a re-run of *The Beverly Hillbillies!*)

The act of fishing must involve a fish, a fisherman and a fishing pole of some kind. A dude casting a line into a fishless backyard swimming pool is not fishing.

A final thought on *Ready! Set! Go!*

After many years in the industry, I was having coffee with a C-suite executive to share with him how we help people. He was an ideal person to visit with, or so I thought. We chatted for fifteen minutes, during which time I showed him how we help people prepare to retire the way they always dreamed of retiring. He was attentive, involved and a great person to interact with throughout our visit. He was, frankly a great conversationalist. All signs led me to believe he would want to see the rest of the story. But that's not what happened.

You see, for years I would connect over coffee, enjoy some meaningful small talk, then transition immediately into showing the person I was with how we help people prepare for the retirement they always dreamed of living.

The initial conversation we've dubbed *So what?* is crafted to create curiosity and put in the mind of the other person a big fat *Hmm...* about their own retirement picture.

We set the hook simply by asking, "Can you think of any reason why you wouldn't want to see the rest of the story?"

Their response had always been, "No."

No is a great response, the one we want to hear. In other words, when they say no, they're saying no, I can't think of any reason why I wouldn't want to see the rest of the story.

And why not? This 20-30-minute conversation is focused on you, your world, and what matters to you. The opening conversation is heavily focused on the *attraction* phase of the *three-part conversation formula* outlined in this book. Asking the rest-of-the-story question is a terrific way of seeing just how attracted the person is to the subject matter of the conversation. When we hear, "No." we know they are curious and interested in seeing more. The great news is that in our experience most people are intrigued, curious and quite interested in chatting again to see how the *Hmm...* resolves itself. *Most* people.

But not that day.

Instead of agreeing to get back together to see the rest of the story, this wonderful gentleman very politely said, "I appreciate everything you have shown me over the past fifteen minutes or so. It's wonderful. Actually, quite impressive. However, there's one problem. You see, Dean, I have no plans to ever retire. I love what I do and I see myself doing this for a really long time. In fact, my dad is eighty-two and still goes into the office every morning. He's not retired and since he's always been my hero, I see myself doing the same thing."

I was surprised. Yet, his response made for one of the best lessons of my entire career. I had assumed he wanted to retire. I assumed everyone did. But not everyone does. Most do, just not everyone. Since then, I have tweaked the very beginning of my initial conversation by simply inserting my point-blank question we unpacked earlier in *Part 3 Go!* ("I'm curious, do you want to retire someday?")

There you have it. Three steps. *Ready! Set! Go!* Together, these three steps are designed to attract the person you are interacting with into a conversation that either leads to engagement or not. Just as a fish sees your lure, swims a bit closer, then chooses to take the lure in, so too do the Ready! Set! Go! questions set you up to attract and engage the people you serve into meaningful conversations.

When you know what you want, and you want it bad enough, you'll find a way to get it.

Jim Rohn

Chapter 7

Yes. No. Maybe.

My sister Julie Harder has been in education her entire adult life. Most of her career has been spent in a classroom as a high school teacher of English and Literature. Julie has also directed theater and supported students in other extracurricular activities. More recently, she moved to the administrative side of the education world, still in the same school, Lincoln East. Julie is the best auntie on the planet, loving on her six nieces and nephews and, more recently, two great-nieces. One of her gifts is knowing what her family wants. Her choice of birthday and Christmas gifts always connects in some way to a hobby or interest of the family member receiving the gift.

My daughter Paige is a beautiful pianist, so Julie often chooses a unique gift that connects to Paige's love of piano. My son Andrew is a runner and a huge Minnesota sports fan, so anything *Twins, Vikings, Wild or Golden Gopher* hits a home run with him. And my son Lucas, a police officer and outdoorsman, grins ear to ear when he gets something from his auntie that he knows will keep him extra warm as he sits twenty feet up in the air on a deer stand in the bitter cold. The point is, Julie is really good at knowing what people want. She isn't just good at giving gifts, she's exceptional at giving *meaningful* gifts. She knows the individual wants of her family members.

Let's spend some time developing a deeper understanding of this principle, as well as how you can use these insights in your own client conversations.

Remember the Step 3 question: "I'm curious, do you want to retire someday?"

Silly, right?

After all, one would think that most people want to retire. However, as you will see below, *how* they respond to the question is like seeing a Christmas present under the tree without wrapping paper on it!

In some of the group training programs we have delivered at The Covenant Group over the years, several participants have first considered this question to be ridiculous. Afterall, it is rare for someone to say, "No, I don't want to retire." As you have already seen, it was hearing "No" during one initial interaction that led me to ask myself a number of questions. Since then, the dialogue has been rewritten to include this point-blank question as part of the standard first conversation.

Though we haven't kept statistics on the response, it is not far-fetched to report that the vast majority of people respond with a hearty, "Heck yeah!" or "Absolutely!" or "You bet I want to retire. In fact, if you can show me how to get there sooner, I'm all ears!"

The only other two responses ever heard are "No" or variations of "Not sure." The "No's" are few and far between, while we hear "Not sure" from 2 or 3 of every 10 asked. For those very few who say no, we immediately pivot to a different conversation; one with its own set of attract and engage pieces meant to help others compel themselves to a meaningful action step. As for the "Not sure" folks, asking a simple follow-up question is all it takes to get to the heart of their want. Here is the simple follow-up question:

"I'm curious, are you not sure you *want* to retire, or not sure you *can* retire?" (By the way, how you say what you say matters too; the emphasis here is on want and can.)

How do most people respond?

"Not sure I can retire."

I hope you are thinking to yourself, whoa, that's amazing! By asking an extremely simple question before we even begin to chat about how we help people, the other party willingly lets us know *what they want* as well as *how they feel about what they want.*

Attracting is focusing on *their* wants, not your own.

We have seen that when clients are given a chance to express what *they* want...well...they do. They share exactly what they want. When you know what the other person wants, your conversations can focus entirely on those wants. It really is a lot like what Zig Ziglar said so many years ago: "You can have everything in life you want, if you will just help other people get what they want!" In other words, help others get what they want *first* and you too will get what you want.

Attraction starts from the outside and moves in. The Covenant Group is where I was first exposed to the idea of identifying Priority Results—the outcomes you want as a result of the business you're building. This lesson from Norm Trainor continues to impact me, even as I write this book.

In our core work with a person who wants to retire, the "want" principle has become a central theme in helping them prepare for the retirement they always dreamed of living—*as defined by them.*

One more thought on this topic of *"want"*. My mom, Carol Harder, has a beautiful touch when she plays piano. As a little girl, she wanted to learn how to play piano. But she had a problem. There was no money for a piano. There was barely money for food. Grandma Hase worked three jobs. Grandpa Hase was not around and then died young, leaving my grandma and her five children in a tough situation. Life was not easy for my mom, her sister Jetta or their brothers Norman, Joel and John. Not easy at all. So, my mom improvised. She cut out white strips of construction paper as well as black strips. Then she taped these strips of paper on a dresser in her bedroom to resemble a full piano keyboard. With musical scores in hand, my mom learned to play the notes, hearing the music in her head. Years later, she was able to begin playing music on a real piano, as well as a multi-keyboard organ.

I'll never forget one Christmas in the 1980's when a baby grand piano arrived at the front door of my parents' house. Mom was speechless. Dad was grinning ear to ear. Today, Mom plays hymns and songs on her piano every day at her home in Mountain Lake. My mom had this deep want as a child, and it still amazes me today what she was willing to do to get what she wanted.

Everyone sees the glory moments, but they don't see what happens behind the scenes.

Allyson Felix

Chapter 8

Scripting the Performance

In the fall of 1983, one of my all-time favorite teachers, Linda Mix, asked me to help her out by reading the part of Prince Charming as other students auditioned for various parts being cast in the fall musical production of *Cinderella*. Little did I know that I was also auditioning. You see, other than a bit part in a community theater production of *Oliver Twist* when I was in elementary school, I had never performed in a play, let alone auditioned for a part. Let's just say that Mrs. Mix wasn't going to take no for an answer. So, as my family and friends sat in the 'red seats' of the Mountain Lake high school auditorium, I made my debut on the same stage where I played basketball, this time wearing white tights in lieu of basketball shorts.

Looking back, unexpected experiences often become the most memorable. The impact of that experience has followed me throughout my life. Two of the most profound impacts on my life can be summed up in a couple of words: *script* and *performance.*

Before my role as Prince Charming, I don't recall ever learning a script. In fact, quite the opposite. I was quick on my feet, an ad-libber, quite comfortable speaking off the cuff. Now, I had to learn a script. But here is what I came to learn about a script. The words of a script are like lumber used to build a house. In a theater production, the words are merely the framework for the story.

The story unfolds as Cinderella, the Fairy Godmother, the Stepmother and Stepsisters, the King and Queen, the Townspeople and even Prince Charming come to life. Each comes to life not simply because the actors speak all the right words, but because they bring feelings, hopes, dreams and emotions to the words. The way each actor moves, stands, stumbles down a set of stairs or dances at the ball matters. Their pacing, the emotion in their voices, the laughter, the sadness, the loudness, the longing, the joy and, of course, that happily-ever-after feeling are just as important as the words first read in Mrs. Mix's third-floor classroom.

You see, when you craft conversations that connect to the life stories of the people you serve, you design words, as well as genuine emotions that allow you to *perform* your role in that very personal story you find yourself invited into. Keep in mind that scripting is normal in nearly any occupation. Musicians script songs. Teachers script lesson plans. Coaches script practices. Doctors script surgeries. Wedding planners script weddings. And funeral directors script funerals.

Salespeople, on the other hand, either fly by the seat of their pants or rely on their go-to sales pitch. How about you consider changing this in your world? Get a feel for how to make scripting a normal part of your sales process.

Let's demonstrate the power of scripting in scenes throughout the sales experience you are creating for the people you serve—your clients. Afterall, you want to *take the stage to create an experience that moves your audience to action.* So, let's get in behind the scenes.

From our years of working with pre-retirees— specifically, those working for others as an employee or a contract-type employee, we know the vast majority of them (well over 90%) have a huge desire to retire someday. In other words, retiring someday is their want. So, crafting conversations focused on their desire to retire is like passing the GO square in the board game Monopoly. This is how three scripted conversations became central to this experience for us.

The three conversations are:

- Conversation 1 – *So what?* (20-30 minutes)
- Conversation 2 – *The Rest of the Story* (45-60 minutes)
- Conversation 3 – *Show Me!* (45-60 minutes)

Conversation 1: So what?
(20-30 minutes)

<u>At the beginning</u> of the *So what?* conversation we follow the same sequence every time. (You learned about it in Chapter 6.)

- *Ready!* (Hey Jerry, do you mind if we jump in?)
- *Set!* (Before we jump in, what were you expecting today?)
- *Go!* (One more quick question...I'm curious if you want to retire someday?)

<u>At the end</u> of the *So what?* conversation you will observe the use of *wouldn't want to* in the question below, followed by the typical response and then the commitment of day and time and the SETTING OF THE EXPECTATION!

"Can you think of any reason why you *wouldn't want to* see the rest of the story?"

Typical reply:

"No. I can't think of any reason."

[Commitment of day and time and SETTING OF THE EXPECTATION]

"Great! Then what do you say we get together same time, same place next week for, let's say, forty-five minutes or so and go through the rest of the story? How does that sound to you?"

Typical reply:

"Sure."

NOTE: Missing any one of these steps is like skipping a step when putting a piece of furniture together. Every step matters.

Conversation 2: The Rest of the Story (45-60 minutes)

At the beginning of the *Rest of the Story* conversation, we go through the *Ready!* and *Set!* steps we just reviewed in the *So What?* conversation.

NOTE: You only go through the Go! Question—the Point-blank question—the FIRST time you interact with someone.

Below is an example of dialogue beginning with some simple small talk that then transitions into the *Ready!* question:

Small Talk example

"How'd your team do this weekend in the playoffs?"

"Susie's team made it to the next round. They are really excited!"

"That's awesome! I'm happy for Susie and her teammates!"

SET! Question

"Before we jump in, what were you expecting this morning?"

They give the *Right* response:

"I thought we were going to go through the rest of the story."

"Great. That's what I thought too. Let's jump in."

OR they give the *Wrong* response:

"I don't really have any expectations."

READY! Question

"Hey Steve, do you mind if we jump in?"
"Sure. Sounds good."

"Well, Jerry, if you recall, when we wrapped up our time together the other day we agreed it would be great to go through what we call 'The rest of the story.' Is that still cool with you?"

"Oh yeah, sure. That sounds good."

"Great. Let's jump in."

OR they give a third response that's still in the *Wrong* category that requires you to adjust on the spot. Let's script out that response too.

"I know you said something about going through the rest of the story together, but I was actually interested in asking you some questions about a money decision I have to make by the end of the week."

"Okay, do you mind telling me about the money decision you have to make by the end of the week?"

"Sure."

They continue on and fill you in. You listen and decide how to proceed. Ultimately, what you want to do is help them with their decision. At the same time, be mindful of how this isolated decision potentially fits into your rest of the story. You want to return to the rest of the story by regaining permission to jump back into it once you deal with their specific money decision question. If, there isn't enough time left to go through the rest of the story then you want to say:

"Great. Glad you asked about this money decision and that you now have a direction on how to handle this issue that has a deadline next week. Given we only have about twenty minutes left before you and I both have to run, how 'bout we connect another day to walk through the rest of the story. How does that sound to you?"

"Yep, that sounds great!"

Three different responses.

The first two responses lead you back to the reason you agreed to get back together. The third response has nothing to do with the rest of the story, at least not until you probe more. Perhaps it does connect to what you wanted to help them see. Perhaps not. This is your opportunity to be a hero—not necessarily one with an answer; rather, one willing to immediately hear them, leading you to immediately change your conversation.

What's the point of all this?

Regaining agreement is focused on attracting your client back into the dialogue you want to have, so you continue to be in a position to help them get what they want. When a person throws you a curveball, as in the third response above, it's almost always best to immediately address that curveball. Swinging as though they threw you a fastball, a changeup or some other pitch is a surefire way of losing their trust.

At the end of our *Rest of the Story* conversation you will observe the use of *wouldn't want to* in the question below, followed by the typical response and then the commitment of day and time and SETTING OF THE EXPECTATION!

"Now, maybe you'd like to say, 'Yes, let's do this!' Unfortunately, it doesn't work like that A company first has to say yes, you can do this if you want to. So, can you think of any reason why you wouldn't want to see if this is even possible?"

Typical reply:

   "No. I can't think of any reason why I wouldn't want to at least see if it's possible."

[Commitment to the NEXT STEP]

   "Great! Then, let's take a moment so that I can share with you what this means, as well as what steps we'll take together to see what's possible. How does that sound to you?"

Typical reply:
   "Sure."

> NOTE: We then spend a moment dialoguing about the process of finding out their possibilities. They again agree to go through the process, knowing that there still is no ultimate commitment. The purpose of this step is simply to find out what is possible. To give you an example from the real estate world, it's the equivalent of going through the process of pre-qualifying for a mortgage, knowing you don't have to actually buy a house just because you have been approved.

Once there is agreement on the next step, the following words will roll off my lips.

"Steve and Susan, that's great. Jane will be leading the process and you and I will be fully aware of the progress week to week through Jane's Friday email updates. Should anything come up that we need to visit about from your end or ours, we'll just pick up the phone and give a call. Cool?"

"Yep, that's cool!" Susan says.

[Commitment of day and time and SETTING OF THE EXPECTATION]

"Okay, if you aren't wondering, so Dean, how might this look for us?—you should be. So far, we have stayed completely conceptual. You have yet to see your stuff inside of these concepts. So, can you think of any reason why you wouldn't want to see how these concepts may impact your world when you put your own stuff inside the different models and tools?"

"No. That would be great." Susan says.

"Alright! I'll ask Jane to find us another forty-five to sixty minutes in the next couple of weeks so that you can see just what this all may mean to you now, as well as someday!"

> NOTE: Missing any one of these steps is like skipping a step when putting a piece of furniture together. Every step matters.

Conversation 3: Show Me!
(45-60 minutes)

At the beginning of the *Show Me!* conversation, we go through the *Ready! Set!* sequence we revisited in Conversation 1 above and then again in Conversation 2. (Remember: you don't go through the *Go!* step, except in Conversation 1.)

Below is an example of dialogue beginning with some simple small talk, that then transitions to the *Ready!* and *Set!* questions.

Small Talk

Just as in Conversation 2, you begin with some small talk to break the ice. Then you use your *Ready!* question:

"Hey Steve, do you mind if we jump in?"

"Sure. Sounds good."

Then the Set! Question

"Before we jump in today, I just want to make sure you and I are on the same page, Steve. What were you expecting this morning?"

Steve gives the Right response:

"I'm looking forward to you showing us what the concept you shared in 'the rest of the story' looks like for Susan and me."

"Great. That's what I was planning on too. So, let's jump in?"

At the end of our *Show Me!* conversation you will observe the use of *wouldn't want to* in the question below, followed by the typical response and then the commitment of day and time and SETTING OF THE EXPECTATION!

Notice that there is some very important dialogue to frame the next scene—the 4th conversation.

"How do you feel about all of this, Susan and Steve?"

"I feel great," says Susan. "For the first time, I feel like we are making decisions about our future where we understand how the pieces are meant to fit together. What about you honey?"

"I agree," says Steve. "I'm really glad we have had these conversations. I'm hoping the process we are going through works out well for us."

"That's great feedback," I say. I too hope the outcome of the process is favorable. As you know, it's likely to be several weeks yet before we know the outcome of the process. It also makes sense for us to continue chatting about all of this, given much of what you have come to see is completely new to you, as it was completely new to me a couple of decades ago.

So, this is what I suggest. How about we connect in a couple of weeks or so to simply visit about what we have already been visiting about? The purpose of chatting next time would be for you to ask or share anything you want to visit about related to our first three conversations. This is a different way of thinking.

So, I'm the first to realize it takes time to get your head and feelings around all the thoughts we have been walking through. I simply want you to feel the freedom to ask any question, push back on any idea, concept or principle we have surfaced. If you have read anything you feel contradicts what we have been chatting about, I encourage you to share that. Let's visit about it. All of it. At the end of the day, you will decide for yourselves if what you are doing already is the best path to take or if the concepts we have surfaced together are the better path for you.

So, can you think of any reason why you wouldn't want to connect again in a couple of weeks or so, simply to revisit anything we have touched on up to this point?"

"Actually Dean, that would be great" Steve says. "We get it, and you have been very helpful. It isn't something we have seen before so we appreciate your offer to get together again to help us gain an even greater understanding and comfort so that when we say, 'Let's do this!' we say it because we really want to do it."

"Awesome! Absolutely awesome! Jane will help us figure out a time that works for the three of us to connect. Looking forward to seeing what questions and thoughts you have next time we chat. See you soon."

NOTE: Missing any one of these steps is like skipping a step when putting a piece of furniture together. Every step matters.

That's it!

Here's the Big Idea

Three conversations that look a lot like three scenes in a live theatre production.

Three scenes that use the same *Ready!* question.

Three scenes that use the same *Set!* question.

Three scenes that each use the same *wouldn't want* to question format for setting expectations for the next conversation.
Three interconnecting scenes:

- Without Scene 1, Scene 2 makes no sense
- Without Scenes 1 & 2, Scene 3 makes no sense
- Without Scenes 1, 2 & 3, Scene 4 makes no sense

When you look behind the scenes you see the effort it takes to make the performance memorable. Yep, it isn't easy. Yep, it's going to take effort. Yet it is so worth it in the end!

Pass GO!

Regaining agreement on something you already agreed to kicks off the crafting the client conversation cycle. Before you dismiss this thought as unnecessary, please keep reading. Regaining agreement is not engaging your client; it is, rather, re-attracting your client to a point of engagement. The best example I have to offer from my own experience is observing people who date, then marry. During the dating phase of their relationship, it's not uncommon to overhear one say to the other, "Do you remember what we wanted to do tomorrow night?"

"I thought we were going out to dinner. Is that what you're thinking?"

"Yep, sure is."

"Where would you like go? You name the place! I know I'll love it!"
When they pick a spot, they do, in fact, love it, no matter where it is. The conversation is lively and fun. They return home feeling great about the evening.

Now, fast forward to the sixth year of marriage, or the third, or even the third month:

"Hey, let's go out to dinner Friday. I was thinking of that Greek restaurant I love. What do you say?"

"What? You know I can't stand Greek food. I'd rather go to that Mexican place I love on Main Street."

"No way! I don't mind Mexican food, but only if we go to that place on the edge of town."

"Well, it doesn't matter what I say. We'll go

wherever you decide anyway."

They end up compromising and going to an Italian restaurant. The food is fine, while the interaction is mostly silent.

So, what's different?

The early courtship scene has clear Attract and Engage moments, while the second scene lacks virtually any attraction moments and is all about engaging on one person's terms with little care for what the other person wants. The latter sounds a lot like a pitch!

The second scene reminds me of typical sales presentations, where the salesperson is more concerned about pitching their idea, product or service, than they are about first getting on the same page.

In crafting the client conversation, it can go a long way to think about your relationship with your client as one where you are always in the dating phase, even if that person has been a client for ten or twenty years. Seek to attract people you have the privilege of intersecting with in life. In doing so, focus on having meaningful conversations that are geared toward their wants. When you do that, most of the time you too get what you want.

Success is getting what you want. Happiness is wanting what you get.

Dale Carnegie

Chapter 9

WHaa

One of my buddies from Mountain Lake has influenced this next section in a big way. Marty Espenson is a corn and soybean farmer in Bingham Lake, Minnesota. Marty has a wisdom about him that exceeds his age. As long as we have been friends, Marty has had a way of knowing what to say, when to say it and who to say it to. I've watched Marty and his wife Patty navigate both business and life decisions as well as anyone I know. The two lower case letters in WHaa are a tribute to Marty and his uncanny ability to zig when it is more popular to zag and to zag when most others zig.

Before we define and understand the WHaa technique, I want to share a story that has left an imprint on me for years. I don't know who to give the credit to, as I don't recall when and where I first heard this story.

Imagine you just bought a house. You have been looking forward to hanging your favorite picture above the fireplace in the living room. The picture is quite heavy, a good forty pounds. You're smart enough to know you need to put an anchor in the wall so the heavy-duty nail you're going to use doesn't tear out of the sheetrock when your picture is placed on the nail. You need to drill a 3/8-inch hole in the drywall before pushing in the anchor. The problem is you don't have a 3/8-inch drill bit. So you head to the hardware store. When you walk in you're not sure where to look for drill bits, so you ask for help. A fine, older gentleman obliges, taking you back to the section with drill bits. You look around and see a sign that reads: If you're looking to buy a hole, you've come to the right place!

The point is rather obvious when you pause to think about it. You use a drill bit to make a hole in the wall so you can then push an anchor into the hole. You really don't want a drill bit. Nope, you really want a hole! If you push this word picture further, you really aren't in the market for a hole in the wall either. Nope, what you really want is to hang your favorite picture on the wall so you can enjoy its beauty. The drill bit is simply a necessary tool for getting what you really want. And that's why life is really about wants, not needs.

The Want–Have–align–adjust (WHaa) technique has the potential to radically change your own selling experience. Let's break down the four elements of this technique so you can see how you too may change the selling experience for the people you serve, as well as change the experience for yourself.

Want

Wants are where you start when it comes to helping people. I'm completely convinced this is true. In the sales world, my wants get in the way of your wants. You have just read the hole story. You start with identifying what the hole is for the person you are wanting to help. Zig Ziglar famously said, "If you help enough people get to the top, you'll get to the top too." So, to paraphrase Zig, if you help enough people get what they want, you'll get what you want too! Knowing what somebody wants isn't complicated. How simple can it be? Below are a handful of examples.

"I'm curious, do you want to retire someday?"
"Yes! Absolutely!"

"I'm curious, do you want to sell your house and move before summer starts?"
"Yes, we do."

"Do you want to be able to play tennis again this year?"

"Yes. I really do. I want this knee healed".

"Do you want to hang that picture over the fireplace?"
"No. I want to hang the picture over the couch."

Notice how each question is a direct one. There is little to no room for misinterpretation. A direct question is absolutely appropriate when you want to know someone else's want.

Have

Have's are all the relevant bits of information that connect to the Want. Think about hanging the picture on the wall above the fireplace. Rather than writing out descriptive sentences, let's list a bunch of words and you make the connections.

> Forty pounds. Drywall. Anchor. Hole. Drill bit. Nail. Hammer. Glass of milk. Lawn mower. Dust. Wood floor. Paper sack. Picture wire. Light switch.

Most of the items are relevant. Some are not. By the way, the light switch is one of the relevant items if the light switch ends up behind the picture or if you need to hang the picture while it's dark in the room. The lawn mower, dust, wood floor and glass of milk are nonsense. The point is the Haves are not just the obvious, like the anchor and the drill bit. They include items that make it possible to do what you want to do.

a – align

Do your Haves align with your Wants? When you're hanging a picture you need all the relevant pieces to finish the job. You could have everything except a light bulb that works in the room. It's rather impossible to properly hang a picture in the dark. Another way to think about this is to create scenarios, given the pieces you have. Can you effectively create the outcome you want if you use only the pieces you have and you continue to use them as you have been doing? If your Haves provide the outcome you Want, then you are aligned. If you find yourself falling short in providing the outcome you want, however, you can only conclude that your Haves do not align with your Want.

- If you have a ½" drill bit, instead of the necessary 3/8" drill bit, you are not aligned.
- If you have a 3/8" hole but no anchor, you are not aligned.
- If you have a 3/8" hole, an anchor but no picture wire, you are not aligned.

a – adjust

Naturally, when your Wants and Haves do not align, you must adjust what you Have so that your Haves align with your Wants. That is the simple framework of WHaa. Hopefully, you're wondering, what does it mean for me? I want to share a personal story to help you see what it may mean for you.

The Mountain Lake golf course opened in 1971. My parents were founding members, as well as terrible golfers. When I say terrible, I can recall my dad's buddies often saying, "Go ahead Don, you can just pick it up if you want!" And my dear mom, she wasn't meant to be a golfer either. But, had they not joined the course, our family would not have been introduced to the game of golf at such a young age. My brother Greg is still an amazing stick. Phil, second in the family, is a natural and he still plays now and again. My sister Julie got Mom and Dad's golf talent. I have never been as good as my brother Greg, although I've had my moments.

Over the past couple years, I have enjoyed taking golf lessons for the first time in well over thirty-five years. For those of you who play, what I'm about to share with you will come as no surprise, while those of you unfamiliar with the game will likely pick up the principle.

Let's start with a very basic description of the object of playing a hole of golf. The object is to hit a little white ball using one of fourteen golf clubs into a 4.25" golf cup in the fewest number of strokes. The first shot is taken from the tee box, the golf cup is located on the green, while the space between the tee box and the green is called the fairway. Of course, there are water hazards, sand traps, boundaries that, if crossed, cause your ball to be out-of-play, as well as other obstructions like trees, bushes, long grass and even big rocks.

So, what's the point? When strategizing how you will play the hole, you start with the end in mind—getting the ball in the hole. So, in order to set yourself up for the best possible outcome—the best scoring opportunity— you play the hole backwards in your mind. This helps you choose how to best set yourself up for the next shot. Golf is a great game of strategy and execution. You need both strategy and execution to score well.

Many casual golfers play from the tee to the green. In other words, they simply whack away in hopes of hitting the ball as far as they can. Eventually the ball will get to the hole. However, even an average golfer who hits the ball decently will struggle to score well if strategy is not a part of the game.

I learned as a teenager to play from the green to the tee. This incorporates strategizing how to position yourself for the next shot, instead of focusing on simply making a good shot. You can hit the ball solid and far, while putting yourself in a bad position for your next shot. I didn't realize until a few years into my sales career that sales is not that different from golf—you start with the end in mind in both cases.

Some have a tendency to believe that when they meet somebody in a sales setting they simply fire their best sales lines and hope that something will stick. This can work from time to time; however, it certainly isn't my cup of tee (*wince*).

One of the best lessons I learned was the result of a test I put myself through on that charming little 9-hole course I grew up on many years ago. I had always played a round of golf with a full set of clubs; fourteen, to be exact. However, on this day I grabbed my 7-iron, wedge and putter setting out on the course with a friend. At that time in my life I was consistently shooting 39-43 on the par 36 9-hole course. That day I shot a 42. Yep. With a 7 iron, wedge and putter. So, what was the test?

I had listened to a speaker around that time who shared the idea that you don't always have to take risk to get reward. This was a new concept to me. I had been taught that to get more reward, I had to be willing to take more risk. The test that day on the golf course was to not take risk. I hit my 7-iron consistently 150-160 yards, was deftly accurate with my wedge from around a hundred yards and in, and that day my putter was reliable on the green. I hit every fairway that day, lost no balls and hit no hazards or traps. I chose to play with only three clubs that day and ended up carding a score of 42, a score similar to a round when I carried all fourteen clubs with me on the course. To this day, my 3-club round is one of the most memorable I've ever played.

When you play golf from the green to the tee, you play with the end in mind. Similarly, you craft the client conversation from the end to the beginning. How do you ultimately want each conversation with this person to play out?

When you help people get what they want, by designing your conversations to start at the end point— the implementation of a solution—and then backward to the initial conversation, you position yourself for good things to happen for the person you are serving, as well as yourself. If you get this sequencing right as you design your conversations around helping people get what they want, your world of helping people will look radically different when compared to what you may be doing today.

Don't focus on the problem, focus on the purpose.

Bo Sanchez

Chapter 10

P-PASS

"Define the problem!" I would say.

Yes, that was my knee-jerk response for much of my life when asked, "What's the first step in problem-solving?" Though many problem-solving methods and techniques continue to teach defining the problem as the first step, I no longer believe that.

I've not written a book prior to this one. It became clear early on that I didn't know how to go about writing a book. My good friend Jones Loflin has authored multiple books, including the award-winning *Juggling Elephants*, co-authored with Todd Musig.

Jones—yes, my friend with two last names—shared some thoughts with me about writing books and his advice was helpful. Another good friend, Jayme Feary, also gave me some pointers, as he too has penned books. Both Jayme and Jones challenged me to simply start writing. And so, I did. I wrote. But I struggled to put down thoughts that were connected. So, I stopped. The advice from my friends was extremely helpful because they challenged me to start writing. Had they not challenged me to start writing, I would likely have never stumbled into a conversation with my friend Dr. Keita Demming.

The breakthrough for me was a conversation I had with Keita, a brilliant thought leader with The Covenant Group. Keita and I partner on a number of projects associated with The Covenant Group, which led us to chat one day about my desire to write a book. Drawing from the WHaa technique fleshed out in Chapter 9 of this book, I knew:

- I WANT to write a book.
- I HAVE no idea how to go about writing a book.
- My WANT and HAVE do not ALIGN.

In my mind, my problem was that I didn't know *how* to write a book. I had attempted writing numerous times over the previous two decades, with nothing to show for what were oftentimes simply Hail-Mary attempts. I was stuck on the problem of not knowing *how* to write a book.

That day, as Keita and I were having a chat, he simply asked, "What do you want your readers to take away from your book? What do you want to message to others through your book? Dean, what's the purpose of the book?" With little hesitation, I said, "When relationships matter, so too do conversations." In other words, I wanted the readers of my book to see that conversations are central to meaningful, productive interactions in the world of sales. I wanted to re-direct well-intentioned "pitchers" to become "skilled chatters."

Keita encouraged me to make an outline built around that one thought, including three key sub-messages related to that one statement, along with three additional details associated with the three key sub-messages. A couple of weeks later, I presented a 12-dot outline to Keita that was focused on one thought: *When relationships matter, so too do conversations.* The twelve dots quickly came to life when I became clear on the purpose of the book—the message—and stopped fixating on how to write a book.

It's true I didn't know *how* to write a book. And given that this is my first book, I'm by no means an expert on how to write one now. That said, solving the problem of not knowing how to write a book became manageable only because I first defined the purpose—the message I wanted to share through the book.

Let's jump back to the personal finance space and break down the P-PASS technique by focusing on commonly held perceptions within the context of the four parts of P-PASS.

P – PURPOSE

The audience: a person or couple desiring to retire someday.

The Perception

- The purpose of saving money for the long-term is retirement.
- The purpose of saving money for the long-term is peace of mind.
- The purpose of saving money for the long-term is security.

The Reality

- The purpose of saving money for the long-term is to create an income stream in retirement so you can live the way you want to live—as defined by you.

Perception vs. Reality

The Perception

Think about someone who saves money into a retirement plan. To many, the perceived purpose of putting money into a retirement plan may be:

- to get a match
- to defer income
- to defer income taxes
- to build wealth
- to _____ (you fill in the blank)

The Reality

When you start by focusing on the want of the person you are serving ("I want to retire someday.") the purpose of saving money for retirement becomes quite clear. The purpose is to create an income stream from the retirement plan that helps you live the kind of retirement life you dream of living someday.

This is the Purpose.

P - PROBLEM

The Perception

- The problem is that I don't know how much money I'll need so I can retire.
- The problem is that I don't know how tax law changes will affect my retirement.
- The problem is that I don't think I'm saving enough money.

The Reality

The problem is that you cannot answer two questions the day you retire:

- How long will you live?
- How will your retirement savings actually perform throughout your retirement years?

Perception vs. Reality

The issues referenced above under *The Perception* are real. The items listed under *The Reality* speak to the heart of the conundrum all retirees face. Not knowing how to answer these two questions is what typically drives you to the conclusions falling under perception. Until you define the real problem—your inability to answer the two impossible questions—the other questions are mere distractions.

A.S. – ATTEMPTED SOLUTION

The Perception

- The attempted solution is to build a pile of money big enough to not run out when you retire.
- The attempted solution is to be in a lower tax bracket.
- The attempted solution is to take out just enough, so you don't run out.

The Reality

The attempted solution may answer the question, how much can you take out, so you don't run out? However, the majority of people don't have the capacity for building a big enough pile of money (retirement savings) that allows them to live the life they've always dreamed of living through their retirement years simply by taking just enough out so they don't run out.

Perception vs. Reality

The attempted solution may resolve the two impossible questions. However, what if it also creates the unintended consequence that you will not be able to live the way you dreamed of living?

S –SOLUTION

The Perception

- The solution is to save even more money.
- The solution is to take even more risk.
- The solution is to work even longer.
- The solution is to lower your expectations about the life you have always dreamed of living in retirement.

Test this out. Search in a web browser the phrase *How to close my retirement income gap.* Look for the four perceived solutions listed above. I would love to hear what you found. (Text me at 317- 659-3020.)

The Reality

The solution is a retirement income strategy that provides you with the income you want so you can live the lifestyle you desire without the fear of running out of money someday. It must be designed differently than the attempted solution.

Perception vs. Reality

The *solution* must fulfill the *purpose* of living the way you want to live throughout your retirement years without running out of money. You do this by resolving the *problem* (the two impossible questions) and also overcoming the *unintended consequence* of the attempted solution.

This is not a book about how to create a retirement income strategy that allows you to live the way you want to live from the day you retire. You have likely picked up that our firm does indeed help people resolve this conundrum. This is not the place, however, to dive into that topic. We are simply using pieces of the conversations we have with the people we serve to help unpack various techniques and methods highlighted in this book, including the technique we have coined P-PASS.

Both the *P-PASS* and *WHaa* techniques are useful when crafting your client conversations. The two techniques feed off one another, much like incorporating the plumbing and electrical components into a house build. You need both. It's tough to work your way around a functional bathroom that's pitch dark. At the same time, it's equally difficult to bathe in a brightly lit bathroom while running a garden hose from your neighbor's outdoor faucet, through your own house and into your bathroom. Both techniques, *WHaa* and *P-PASS,* provide critical frameworks when it comes to crafting your client conversations.

Using WHaa and P-PASS together is key to helping people find their own realities and seeing a way through the pieces that seem impossible to resolve. These two techniques are foundational in attracting and engaging people you can help. When the people you serve feel heard, educated, and empowered, they are compelled to consider choices, make decisions, and pursue directional changes.

Helping others see themselves standing in the fork in the road is a lot different than telling someone they are at a fork in the road. You're not here to pick a fight; quite the contrary. You're here to help people see their reality. (Remember the sleep study guy?)

Hint: Don't start your conversations by debating variables nobody controls. You may think the tax rates in ten years are going to be x and I may think they're going to be y. At the end of the day, neither of us knows what the tax rates will be in ten years. So what's the point in debating tax rate changes? At best, we can agree tax rates will go up or down over the next decade. Don't debate reasonable hypothetical rate of return assumptions, or assumed inflation rates, or future interest fluctuations. Your guess is as good as mine. Neither of us really has a clue. Rather than debating a topic neither of us can ultimately prove right or wrong, you should instead start by giving the other person the benefit of the doubt that every assumption you cannot control goes your way. Giving people the benefit of the doubt that all the things they don't control go their way is a huge step in helping people see themselves at the fork in the road, rather than telling them they are at a fork in the road.

Taking several dozen golf lessons over the past two years has proven this truth out. During one lesson, I was convinced my take-away and backswing club path was in one spot, while my patient coach, Clint, said, "No Dean, it's not. Your brain may think it's there, but I can tell you it's not." Rather than debating with me, he brought up the video of the swing, from front, side and back cameras. After playing the video in slow motion a few times it was painfully obvious that Clint was one hundred percent right and I was completely off my rocker.

In that moment I saw myself standing in the fork in the road.

Clint was having me adjust my backswing to create a different club path back to the ball so that, ultimately, the shot would end in a slight draw rather than an all too typical fade off to the right. Seeing the video proof was all it took to talk to my own brain. I was immediately compelled to change because I wanted a different result. After several more swings, I began to see the ball flight draw in mid-air. To Clint's credit, he didn't get into a debate with me. He simply allowed me to see that if I kept doing what I was doing the results would continue to be what I would not want.

Focusing the conversation on the assumptions and circumstances you have no control over typically leads to a stalemate of some sort. However, when you see with your own eyes that if you keep doing what you're doing that you don't stand a chance of getting what you want, you suddenly become all ears and eyes to hear and see how else you might go about getting what you want. You return to that spot—the fork in the road.

P-PASS is indeed one of the most profound and helpful guideposts in our work in helping others get what they want.

It'll be Okay.

Donald J. Harder

Chapter 11

Words Matter

Dad was a man of few words. Yet when he spoke, his words had impact. Some of you may recall a famous line spoken in an old EF Hutton television commercial: "When EF Hutton talks, people listen."

That was Dad. He couldn't tell a joke to save his life, nor was he much of a storyteller. But what he lacked in senseless chatter, Dad more than made up for in simple wisdom. He passed away in 1997, yet his life lessons continue to encourage and challenge me today. I'd like to close out our time together with one of the most meaningful lessons I learned from my dad, Donald Harder.

I vividly recall a moment with Dad when I was twenty-five—that's thirty years ago, as I pen these words. Jackie and I had been married only a year or so and we were in hot pursuit of our first home. We had been renting an apartment for a little over a year and felt like we were throwing money away. After looking at a couple of dozen homes and finding nothing to our liking, we shifted gears and started looking at building a home.

We found an opportunity that was quite a financial stretch for us; however, on paper we could make it work. Before pulling the trigger, Jackie and I thought it would be good to talk it over with Dad to see what he thought. After sharing with him our new direction of building a home rather than buying an existing one, along with the little detail that a new home build would come with a $150,000 price tag, compared to the $70,000 - $100,000 for the homes we had looked at, Dad asked a simple question.

"You have shared that when you start your family you want to have the option of being a one-income family. Is that still what you want?"

"Yeah Dad, that's still what we want."

"If you build this house, will you still have the option of being a one-income family when you start having kids?"

"No, probably not right away, but hopefully later," I said.

"Why is it that you want to be in a house so badly?"

"Because we are tired of throwing rent money away," I said.

Then, some of the most meaningful and impactful words hit my ears, words that drive my decision-making to this day.

"Rent buys you time," Dad said. "Time to make a wise decision, rather than an unwise one. You said you wanted to have the option for Jackie to stay home once you start your family. Sounds to me like building this house takes that away from you. But, it is your decision to make."

Jackie and I found ourselves standing in the fork in the road.

We passed on building or even buying a house at the time. In fact, we didn't buy our first house until more than a year later, when we 'fell into' an opportunity to buy an amazing starter home for $93,000. And we did become a one-income family—our choice— with no regrets about doing so.

You see, words matter. And, as my dad proved so many times in my life, it doesn't take a lot of words to help others get what they want. Little did I know that my dad—a turkey, corn and soybean farmer all his life—

was planting seeds in me for a book I would write someday. Throughout my life I have desired to live out the wisdom Dad shared, wisdom he was careful to never cram down my throat.

One final bit of wisdom that comes from my dad is bitter-sweet at best. In January of 1997, Dad was taken to the Mayo Clinic in Rochester, Minnesota where he would later pass away on February 5. Less than three years earlier, my dad and I laid side by side in hospital beds waiting to be wheeled into our respective surgical rooms for a kidney transplant procedure. We both were blind as a bat, so without our eyeglasses on we were placed so that our faces were no more than eighteen inches from one another as we chatted a bit before going into our separate operating rooms. My dad thanked me for my desire to give him one of my healthy kidneys. Then he said, "It'll be ok."

I didn't think much of it then, given I was not anxious or worried about giving up something God had given me at birth—my kidney. Any anxiousness I had then was directed at Dad being able to keep the kidney without his body rejecting it. It was to the latter thought that Dad responded by saying, "It'll be okay."

In the days leading up to the fifth of February, it became quite apparent that, apart from a miracle from God, my dad was going to die. I can't say with certainty that the last words I remember hearing my dad say were *It'll be okay*, but I can say that hearing those words as I said goodbye to him have been an anchor to hold on to when the water has been choppy in my own journey.

As I think back to my own life's journey, I have often not listened well to perhaps my dad's most simple words: "It'll be ok." So, I choose to end these pages with this very personal memory so that I may reframe why I have chosen to write a book on conversational selling.

When relationships matter, so too do conversations.

Lying beside my dad in the surgical prep room is one of my most sacred memories. So too are the several chats we shared in his final weeks in Rochester. But those conversations are especially sweet because of the hundreds—no, thousands—of conversations we shared when I was a kid, a teenager, a young adult, a newly married husband and a father to his grandchildren, Andrew and Lucas, and eventually Paige who was born seven weeks after Dad died. I've chosen to write this book on conversational selling because I see the art of simple, genuine, other-focused conversations becoming a lost art. Embracing the ideas and techniques in the pages of this book is in many ways my tribute to Dad's "It'll be ok."

It'll be ok if you help the other person get what they want, but you don't actually get what you want. Sales should first be measured by how big a difference you make in the lives of others; in other words, how many other people's wants you help to make reality. I certainly want you to be even more successful than you already are by using what is shared freely in this book. I really do. I also want you to experience a different journey. A journey focused on helping, not pitching.

My challenge to you now that you have finished this book is for you to test the guidelines, principles, techniques, tips, hints and bits of wisdom offered here to begin crafting your own client conversations. Why? So that you can help others get what they want and because I know that, along the way, you'll get enough of what you want.

Acknowledgments

You would not be reading or listening to this book if a series of conversations hadn't taken place with a few important people in my life. There is no way I can capture all the names, so I choose to personally thank Keita, John, Norm, Joel, Jane, and six others. Keita Demming is the one who struck the match that started this firestorm in me. Thank you my friend for stoking the fire throughout these past several years as you helped me bring this book to life. My on-the-job book writing teacher was John Donnelly, the editor of *Stop Pitching!* You are the ideal mix of technical skill and masterful artistry when it comes to using your gift of helping others take a book from an idea to...well...a book. Norm Trainor is a business coach and has been my coach for nearly eight years. He is a master at helping people get what they want. I wanted to write a book and Norm helped me make it happen. You are a remarkable man doing remarkable things, Norm. Yet it is the friendship we have forged over the years that I actually cherish the most. Joel Weldon is more than a Hall of Fame speaker; he is also perhaps the greatest speaking and communication coach on the planet. Hiring you to coach me in my speaking and presentation skills just two years ago, Joel, has in no small part seen this book become a reality. Jane Perkins, my long-time colleague and personal friend to Jackie and me, pulls the strings in my business life. You too are gifted in a unique way, Jane, to help this Minnesota kid pursue and capture his dreams. Authors also oftentimes thank their families. I too want to thank Jackie, Andrew and Becca, Lucas and Paige and Paige (Yes, there are two!), as well as Sophia and Samantha. There is no other relationship in life that matters more than family. You know that I have not always lived out the lessons shared in this book at home. So, it is the grace you have given me that makes me want to say one more time, when relationships matter, so too do conversations. Thank you for having the good, bad and the ugly conversations with me through the years.

Index

Carol Harder 93

Cotton System 79

Crysteel Manufacturing 19

Donald Harder 135

Dr. Keita Demming 46, 124

EF Hutton 135

Eric Hagman 11

Indianapolis 500 65

Jane Perkins 73

Jayme Feary 124

Jon Eric Hase 83

Jones Loflin 123

Lake Crystal 19

Linda Mix 95

Marty Espenson 113

Mountain Lake 12, 21, 55, 93, 95, 113, 118

Nancy A. Noel 39

Norm Trainor 23, 46, 92

Pablo Picasso 39

Priority Results 92

Ron Harder 78

Speedway, Indiana 65

Sylvia Ekstedt 12

The Covenant Group 23, 24, 46, 57, 81, 90, 92, 124

TIDADS 41, 42, 45, 47

Todd Musig 123

Tom Appel 12

Top-20 13

University of Minnesota 68

Verlyn Fast 55

Wayne Cotton 79

Wilbur Shaw 65

Zig Ziglar 54, 92, 115

About the Author

Dean Harder splits time between Indiana and Florida, after living the first 43 years of his life in Minnesota. Since 1998, the heart of his business is helping people spend and enjoy as well as share their wealth with others. This farm boy at heart has been married to a farm girl for over 30 years and counts family as his greatest blessing.

Made in the USA
Las Vegas, NV
30 August 2022

54399263R00090